One of our world's great problems is ego-centric, self-serving leadership—leaders who think people exist for their benefit, instead of vice versa. In stark contrast, Jesus modeled servant leadership, leading by example. He said, "I came to serve, not to be served." Now, two thousand years later, Jesus has over 2.1 billion followers, which makes Him the undisputed greatest leader of all time. No one else comes close! This is why you need to know how to lead like Jesus. He is the only flawless example. That's why you should read this book!

Rick Warren
Author, *The Purpose Driven Life*
Named one of "America's Twenty-five Best Leaders" (*U.S. News and World Report*)

I had the pleasure of hosting at our church one of Ken Blanchard and Phil Hodges's Lead Like Jesus Celebrations. What an impactful day that was for those who participated. I know they will never think about leadership in the same way again. Reading *Lead Like Jesus* will provide you with that kind of experience. Don't miss learning from the greatest leadership role model of all time.

Bob Russell, Senior Pastor, Southeast Christian Church

Ever since writing *Leadership by the Book* with Ken Blanchard and Phil Hodges, I've watched them grow in their depth of understanding of what the Bible reveals about how Jesus would have us lead others. The best thinking the Lord has revealed to them, to this point, can be found in this book. If you want to be the servant leader that Jesus mandated His followers to be, then read *Lead Like Jesus*. It will change your life and the lives of people you are able to influence.

Bill Hybels, Senior Pastor, Willow Creek Community Church

You'll find few men better qualified to address this topic than Ken Blanchard. His favorite name is "Jesus" and preferred verb is "lead." Let him do for you what he's done for me and millions of others—help you lead like Jesus.

Max Lucado, Pastor, Oak Hills Church, Best-selling Author

Finally. Finally. Finally. A definitive guide to the connection between our faith and our work—one that is both theoretically elegant and immensely practical. This is, without a doubt, the most important management book I have ever encountered.

Patrick Lencioni, Author, *The Five Dysfunctions of a Team*

Ken Blanchard and Phil Hodges continue to lead us deeper into the gold mines of God's Word to the treasured truth of life. *Lead Like Jesus* promises a refurbishing, applicable perspective from the leader of all time!

Dan T. Cathy, President and COO, Chick-fil-A, Inc.

For those who seek to lead like Jesus, this book is an important reflective tool in helping to better understand—who we are, where we are going, and why it is important for people to follow. It is a reminder to all of us that leadership is only a means. To what end is the ultimate question.

C. William Pollard, Chairman, The Service Master Company

There is no greater leadership model than Jesus, and Blanchard and Hodges have taken years of experience identifying the leadership characteristics of Jesus that will affect your life and leadership. They have have hit the nail on the head with *Lead Like Jesus*.

John C. Maxwell, Founder, INJOY Stewardship Services & Equip
New York Times Best-Selling Author

Millions of people wish everyone could lead like Jesus. Ken Blanchard and Phil Hodges have dedicated their time and energy, insights and professionalism, to make it happen. Read this book and ponder the questions raised, the ideas presented, and ask yourself if you too can take up the challenge in your own life. It's not just what would Jesus *do*, but especially, how would Jesus *lead*? This book will help you find the answers.

Laurie Beth Jones, Author, *Jesus, CEO*; *The Path*; *Jesus: Life Coach*; and *The Four Elements of Success*

Ken has a divine passion for leaders to let Jesus live out His life through them in servant leadership. His book, *Lead Like Jesus*, is an extremely timely book that is both thorough and God-honoring. I highly recommend it to all who lead others.

Henry Blackaby, Author, *Experiencing* God

As I read the compelling words in *Lead Like Jesus*, I found myself nodding enthusiastically and resisting the urge to shout "Amen!" at the turn of each page. Their message—whether we sit in the family room or the board room—is undeniable: Jesus calls us to servant leadership, the essence of who we are in Him and how we demonstrate His love. His command leaves us no choice—and to this I say, "Amen."

Paul J. Meyer, Founder,Success Motivation Institute, Inc. and 40+ companies
New York Times Best-Selling Author

Lead Like Jesus is a gift to the sincere and a beacon of light to the lost. May the knowledge conveyed in this teaching help spread the message of truth around the world. It has spoken to my heart as well as my mind.

Mary Anne Shula, Shula Enterprises

Lead Like Jesus transcends all relationships and cuts to the heart of the matter—leading like Jesus will change you and the lives you touch. Choose this book today to be challenged and motivated to lead at a higher level everywhere! You'll never be or lead the same again!

Marjorie Dorr, Chief Strategy Officer, WellPoint, Inc.

In *Lead Like Jesus* we learn that it is intimacy with Jesus that transforms our lives and leadership. The difference between this and other leaderhip books is that the focus on Jesus encourages the leader to actually learn, grow, and change behavior. There is no more effective way to becoming a great leader.

Vince Siciliano, President, First Pacific Bank

Enlightening, challenging, and convicting—the only complete book on leadership I've ever read. It will be read one hundred years from now.

Charlie "Tremendous" Jones, Executive Books

A path-breaking book in every way. This book shows you how to live your faith in your world—without ducking, without offending. Follow the path and be changed in every way.

Bob Buford, Author, *Halftime and Finishing Well*
Founder, Leadership Network

Lead Like Jesus takes the concept of servant leadership and makes it simple enough to begin implementing it right away. The idea that servant leadership is about the head, the heart, and the hands makes it easy to understand why vision, character, and implementation are each so critical to true leadership performance. Reading this book today will be the first step in making you a better servant leader tomorrow.

Zig Ziglar, Author/Motivational Teacher

LEAD LIKE JESUS

LESSONS FOR EVERYONE FROM THE
GREATEST LEADERSHIP ROLE MODEL OF ALL TIME

Ken Blanchard & Phil Hodges

THOMAS NELSON
Since 1798

NASHVILLE DALLAS MEXICO CITY RIO DE JANEIRO BEIJING

Published in Nashville, Tennessee, by Thomas Nelson. Thomas Nelson is a registered trademark of Thomas Nelson, Inc.

Thomas Nelson, Inc., titles may be purchased in bulk for educational, business, fund-raising, or sales promotional use. For information, please e-mail SpecialMarkets@ThomasNelson.com.

ISBN 978-1-4003-1420-1 (repackage)

The Library of Congress has cataloged the earlier edition as follows:

Blanchard, Kenneth H.
Lead like Jesus : lessons from the greatest leadership role model of all times / Ken Blanchard and Phil Hodges.
p. cm.
Summary: "Learn how to lead like Jesus, whether in the home, the church, the community, or the marketplace; moving not only from success to significance but taking a step beyond significance—surrender"—Provided by publisher.
Includes bibliographical references.
ISBN 978-0-8499-1872-8 (trade paper)
ISBN 978-0-8499-0040-9 (hardcover)
1. Leadership—Religious aspects—Christianity. 2. Leadership—Biblical teaching. 3. Jesus Christ—Leadership. 4. Bible. N. T. Gospels—Criticism, interpretation, etc. I. Hodges, Phil. II. Title.
BV4597.53.L43B575 2005
253—dc22 2005028427

Printed in the United States of America
12 13 QG 14

Acknowledgments

A book like this always takes a village to write. Besides our three member consultant team of the Father, the Son, and the Holy Spirit, we want to acknowledge the efforts and contributions of the following servant leaders.

Karen McGuire for her gifted contribution of the prayers of leaders and followers and her skillful and loving care in proofreading and editing so the Lead Like Jesus message would be presented just as He would like it.

Avery Willis and Lee Ross, our co-authors of the *Lead like Jesus: Beginning the Journey* study guide, for the many concepts we developed together in that earlier work that also appear in this book.

Phyllis Hendry for faithfully leading the Lead Like Jesus team and always demonstrating Jesus through everyday relationships and assignments.

The Lead Like Jesus team who continually and consistently demonstrate leading like Jesus in everyday tasks both great and small.

Bob Pike for his generosity and support in sharing his great insights, comments, and feedback that provided clarity, direction, and purpose.

Vince Siciliano for his probing inquiries, honest feedback, and contribution to the Exalting God Only concept.

Jack Countryman, who believed in the Lead Like Jesus message early on and published *The Servant Leader* and *Lead Like Jesus: Beginning the Journey* group study.

Tami Heim, whose commitment to Lead Like Jesus fostered our new publishing relationship with Thomas Nelson, Inc.

David Moberg and Mary Hollingsworth, our new W Publishing Group editorial team, for their tireless efforts in the editorial management process.

Nancy Jordan for getting us started pulling manuscripts together and loving every word.

Our spouses, Margie and Jane, for their loving support through our journey of learning to Lead Like Jesus.

Laurie Beth Jones, Rosey Grier, and Phyllis Hendry for sharing their personal stories.

Kevin Small for his feedback and expertise in book contracts and positioning.

We owe a debt of gratitude to a wide variety of Christian writers past and present whose wisdom and concepts have helped shape the Lead Like Jesus message including:

Dallas Willard for his high scholarship and wisdom in calling us into a deeper and more intimate relationship with Jesus.

Henry Blackaby for his unwavering focus on abiding in the heart, mind, and will of God.

Robert S. McGee for his penetrating concept regarding the folly of following "Satan's formula for self-worth being the sum of your performance plus the opinion of others."

Bill Hybels, who was our co-author of *Leadership by the Book* and got us going down this journey of looking at the heart, head, hands, and habits of leading like Jesus.

Contents

To leaders everywhere who go quietly about the day-to-day task of serving others with courage and humility! May the example of Jesus make a difference in your lives and the lives of those you touch.

Introduction

THE LEAD LIKE JESUS JOURNEY

Faith and business. Jesus and parenting.
Personal and professional. Servant and leader.

Seeing those words paired together makes people uneasy. Our sophisticated culture encourages us to draw lines and keep our spiritual lives separate from our secular lives. Faith is only for Sundays or family gatherings, right?

A Word from Ken Blanchard

I, too, once modeled my life after that tired pattern, and I had a generally good, successful life. I had earned full professor with tenure at age thirty-five at the University of Massachusetts. In 1976–77 my wife, Margie, and I went on sabbatical leave. We then decided to stay in California to start our training and consulting company. Blanchard Training and Development was a quick and early success that began to grow in leaps and bounds. But the Lord was not central in my life. It wasn't until the publication of *The One Minute Manager* nationally in 1982 that I began to think about God. That book was so amazingly successful in such a short period of time that even I had trouble taking credit for its success. I began to think somehow it was a "God thing."

Opening my mind to that possibility, the Lord began to send all kinds of believers into my life, starting with my longtime friend and colleague Phil Hodges. Phil and I had met on the bus going to orientation camp at Cornell University in 1957. He had turned his life over to the Lord a few years before, and ever since, he'd been praying for me. When he heard about the success of *The One Minute Manager*, Phil called and said, "Ken, let's take a walk on the beach." During our walk, he said, "Why do you think this book is so successful? Do you think you are smarter or a better writer than other people?" I said, "No, Phil. I think somehow God is involved."

Phil was delighted with my answer and began to give me Christian publications to read. But I was slow to commit. However, the Lord kept on sending me people who pushed me closer to Him, like Norman Vincent Peale with whom I co-authored *The Power of Ethical Management.*[1] Right from the beginning, Norman said to me, "Ken, the Lord's always had you on His team; you just haven't suited up yet."

My journey continued and was further impacted by Bob Buford, author of *Halftime*, and Bill Hybels, founding pastor of Willow Creek Community Church outside of Chicago. With my new spiritual team of Hodges, Peale, Buford, and Hybels, I finally couldn't deny the power of God's grace and the gift that He offers us. I suited up for the Lord.

When I turned my life over to the Lord in the late 1980s, I began to read the Bible. As a behavioral scientist, I went straight to the Gospels—Matthew, Mark, Luke, and John—and the book of Acts because I wanted to know what Jesus did. As I studied those books, I became fascinated with how Jesus transformed twelve ordinary and unlikely people into the first generation of leaders of a movement that continues to affect the course of world history some two thousand years later. I soon became aware that everything I had ever taught or written about effective leadership during the past thirty-five years, Jesus did to perfection, beyond my ability to portray or describe. I realized that Christians have more in Jesus than just a spiritual leader; we have a practical and effective leadership model for all organizations, for all people, for all situations. As a result, Phil Hodges and I co-founded the Lead Like Jesus ministry to inspire and equip people to lead like Jesus and to follow His mandate to be servant leaders.

Our Hope for this Book

We want you to experience Jesus in a whole different way—to grow to trust Him as the perfect One to follow as you seek to lead others. This involves surrendering your life and leadership to Him. The real secret to leading like Jesus is found in Proverbs 3:5–6: "Trust in the LORD with all your heart and lean not on your own understanding; in all your ways acknowledge him, and he will make your paths straight."

Jesus is clear about how He wants us to lead: He asks us to make a difference in our world by being effective servant leaders. It is our prayer and desire that *Lead Like Jesus* will be the beginning of a new and exciting chapter in your personal journey to becoming an effective servant leader. It is designed to guide you in exploring your personal response to Jesus' call to "Come, follow me" and to put into action the principles of servant leadership.

Is this a leadership text for business? Yes. Is this a book to improve personal relationships? Yes. Is this an inspirational guide to a more intimate relationship with God? Yes. Simply put, *Lead Like Jesus* is a tool to help you take God beyond the spiritual compartment of your private spiritual life and to give Him free rein in all your daily actions and relationships, especially your leadership roles. Don't worry if you do not have a formal leadership role as you read this book—think of your relationships to your spouse, kids, friends, co-workers, and colleagues with whom you interact every day. The concepts in this book are not complex but they are challenging. They can be applied at any level of leadership, from the family room to the corporate board room. Don't approach this book as merely an intellectual exercise; take it to heart. We want you to change not only your knowledge, but also your attitudes, actions, and behaviors—your very life! Do you know how long it took Jesus to change His disciples' attitudes and behaviors related to servant leadership? Three years of daily interactions.

We have written this book to influence your daily interactions with others and to transform the behavior of those in your organization or family. This is a tall order. So we suggest the following steps to help you reap the greatest benefits from reading this book:

1. *Begin in prayer*. Ask God to guide you to the truth that will have the greatest impact on improving the way you lead.
2. *Skim through the entire book*. Skim through the book quickly to get a sense of the entire Lead Like Jesus concept. Then, slow down and take your time to study it in-depth.
3. *Read each chapter and underline key thoughts*. Be careful not to underline too much. Only highlight when you encounter

"Aha!" ideas that challenge your leadership behaviors and motives.

4. *Take time to pause and reflect.* Resist the temptation to focus your attention on what other people should do to improve their leadership. Remember, this is about you! After reading each chapter, stop to review your underlined sections and ask yourself, "How could knowing that concept or idea make me a better leader?" Be specific. Jot your ideas in the margin. We have included some "Pause and Reflect" stops in each chapter to give you a chance to let the message permeate your heart as well as your mind.
5. *Summarize your "Aha!" ideas and reflections in a separate journal.* Include action steps and plans on how you can apply what you are learning in your day-to-day life at work or in your family.
6. *Share with others what you have learned.* The best way to learn is to teach. After you have summarized your "Aha!" ideas, organize a meeting of all the people who are impacted by your leadership but have not read this book. Share with them what you have learned and how you intend to apply it. Use your journal as your study guide.
7. *Periodically review your progress in leading like Jesus.* Praise your progress, and redirect your efforts where you think you have lapsed. When you monitor your attempts to lead like Jesus, you will be surprised what God will do through your leadership as you apply these biblical principles. If you want a true picture of how well you are doing in implementing change in your leadership behavior, ask the people you lead for some feedback.

We want you to come to trust Jesus as your leadership role model, so whether you are leading in a business, in a nonprofit organization, in your community, in your church, or in your home, you will make Jesus smile. It is the vision of our Lead Like Jesus ministry that someday, everywhere, everyone will know someone who is leading like Jesus. Join us in our quest!

God bless.

Ken Blanchard and Phil Hodges
Winter 2006

Chapter 1

WHO WILL YOU FOLLOW? HOW WILL YOU LEAD?

The world is in desperate need of a different leadership role model. Pick up any daily newspaper, and you will quickly find examples of abandoned values, betrayed trust, exploitation, and manipulation committed by people of power and influence. Corporate leaders exploit privileges of position, bringing ruin to employees and investors. Meanwhile, citizens of underdeveloped countries languish in poverty and hopelessness in a leadership vacuum. Church leaders experience crises of integrity, compromising their churches and breeding skepticism and disillusionment. Families and personal relationships drift away from mutual commitment and head toward battlegrounds of self-absorbed conflict over rights to individual fulfillment.

In one sense, the leadership model that people often experience is summarized by the popular opinion: "It's all about me." In all kinds of organizations and institutions, the rewards of money, recognition, and power increase as you move up the hierarchy. Self-promotion (pride) and self-protection (fear) are the reigning motivations that dominate the leadership landscape. Many leaders act as if the sheep are there only for the benefit of the shepherd. In personal relationships, leadership expectations of mutual respect, loving care, self-sacrifice, and openness are often undermined when pride, fear, and indifference replace intimacy with isolation. That's the bad news.

The good news is that there is a better way. There is one perfect leadership role model you can trust, and His name is Jesus.

There is a way to lead that honors God and restores health and effectiveness to organizations and relationships. It is the way Jesus calls us to follow as leaders: to serve rather than be served.

As you begin your journey of leading like Jesus, you have to answer the following three key questions, which we will explore in this chapter:

1. Am I a leader?
2. Am I willing to follow Jesus as my leadership role model?
3. How do I lead like Jesus?

Am I a Leader?

Leadership is a process of influence. Anytime you seek to influence the thinking, behavior, or development of people in their personal or professional lives, you are taking on the role of a leader. Leadership can be as intimate as words of guidance and encouragement to a loved one or as formal as instructions passed through extended lines of communication in organizations. Leadership can be nurturing the

Am I a Leader?

Leadership is a process of influence. Anytime you seek to influence the thinking, behavior, or development of people in their personal or professional lives, you are taking on the role of a leader.

character and self-worth in children and promoting greater intimacy and fulfillment in personal relationships, or it can involve distributing diverse resources in an organization to accomplish a specific objective and task.

Each of the following situations describes someone engaged in an act of leadership:

- A mother with a child at any time of day
- A friend who risks alienation to confront a moral failure
- A corporate executive who rejects offers of inside information to gain a competitive edge
- A U.S. Navy SEAL commander who orders his troops into harm's way to succeed in their mission
- A husband and wife who seek mutual agreement on day-to-day finances
- A middle school teacher who excites curiosity in the minds of her students
- A rehabilitation nurse who patiently handles the anger of a stroke victim
- A missionary doctor who refuses to leave his patients to avoid capture by enemy forces
- A local pastor who avoids teaching on controversial issues for fear of rejection
- A high school coach who fails to confront rule violations by his star player

- An adult who provides advice and guidance on living arrangements to his aging parent
- A terminally ill patient who demonstrates grace, confidence, courage, and calm to anxious loved ones
- A local government official who takes an unpopular political stand based on principle
- A dictator who hoards millions of dollars while his citizens are starving

Two things are evident in this list. First, each of these people is a leader because he or she is affecting or influencing others, either in a positive or negative way. This list reveals that some leadership actions are very specific in nature (a dictator hoarding millions), and others are more general (a mother with a child); some are overt (an official taking an unpopular stand), and some are covert (a pastor avoiding teaching on a controversial issue). The actions of a leader that create influence are not always obvious to those being led. We also influence people who may not choose to follow, such as the executive who refuses insider information.

Second, these leaders are involved in making a personal choice about how and to what end they will use their influence. It is the same choice we are all called to make when we exert influence on people: do we seek to serve or to be served? If your driving motivations are self-promotion and self-protection, you will use your influence with others to fulfill these needs. If your actions are driven by service and dedication to a cause or a relationship, then you will model and encourage these values in others.

As you think about the many ways you influence the actions of other people, you can see that you are a leader wherever you go, not just at work. Whether you serve others as parent, spouse, family member, friend, or citizen—or whether you have a leadership title and position like CEO, pastor, coach, teacher, or manager—you are a leader!

As we consider how we can lead like Jesus in our various leadership roles, we need to be aware of the difference between life role leadership and organizational leadership.

Life Role Leadership

Functions in enduring relationships (parent, spouse, sibling, friend, citizen)

Focuses on growing and developing people and supporting mutual commitment in life role relationships

Involves seasons of personal sacrifice to promote the spiritual and physical well-being of others to whom you are bound in an enduring relationship

Is based on duty, honor, and lifelong obligation

Is resilient based on the level of relational commitment

Anticipates love, loyalty, trust, mercy, forbearance, forgiveness, and sacrifice

Is seasonal in levels of influence based on maturity and growth

Values love, compassion, trust, commitment, honesty, and grace

---

Organizational Leadership

Involves positions and titles bestowed at the convenience of the organization to serve the perceived needs and culture of the organization
Measured accountability for long- and short-term results under constant scrutiny by a variety of stakeholders (investors, governing boards, employees, customers, analysts, alumni, unions, regulatory agencies, partners, congregations, constituencies)
At risk based on performance and preferences of governing bodies and stakeholders
Power and influence are prone to conflicting agendas and priorities (finance versus marketing, engineering versus manufacturing, church staff versus lay leadership, staff versus operations)
Sensitive to shifts in organizational structure, standards, and priorities (mergers and acquisitions, reorganizations, outsourcing, and alliances)
Reward delivered in the form of additional power, material rewards, and recognition
Operates in the realm of competition and marketplace standards and biases (globalization, technology, demographics, trends, and fashion)
Values competence, material results, vision, courage, diligence, confidence, conviction, and integrity

The most dramatic difference between life role leadership and organizational leadership involves the permanence of the relationships the leader is trying to influence. Life role leaders function in enduring lifelong relationships as parents, spouses, siblings, friends, and citizens, where duty and obligation cannot be easily relinquished or discarded.

Organizational leaders, on the other hand, operate for a season in an environment of temporary relationships and change. People in positions come and go in organizations for all sorts of reasons. Whom you will be working with or for in a given year can change in an instant! This lack of stability often breeds a degree of reserve and qualified commitment acted out in the arena of competitive office politics.

Most of the leadership that shapes our lives does not come from leaders with titles on an organization chart; it comes from leaders in our daily life role relationships. It is instructive to note that in the early church, a candidate's life role leadership was a prerequisite for assuming organizational leadership. In 1 Timothy 3:1–7, we read:

> Here is a trustworthy saying: If anyone sets his heart on being an overseer, he desires a noble task. Now the overseer must be above reproach, the husband of but one wife, temperate, self-controlled, respectable, hospitable, able to teach, not given to drunkenness, not violent but gentle, not quarrelsome, not a lover of money. He must manage his own family well and see that his children obey him with proper respect. (If anyone does not know how to manage his own family, how can he take care of God's church?) He must not be a recent convert, or he may become conceited and fall under the same judgment as the devil. He must also have a good reputation with outsiders, so that he will not fall into disgrace and into the devil's trap.

One person who exemplified servant leadership in Jesus' life was His mother, Mary. The legacy of obedience, submission, faith, and service that Mary passed on to her son is the subject of a rich heritage of thought that we will not venture to add to at this time. Mary epitomized the essence of a servant heart. In her life role as a mother, she was positioned to have strategic influence on the life and spirit of her child. The relationship between mother and son—between a soul already tested and found willing and one to be nurtured, between spiritual teacher and student—was part of God's plan of preparation for Jesus' season of leadership.

■ **Pause and Reflect**

Take a moment to think about the people who have most influenced your thinking, behavior, and life path. As you recall their names and faces, you will realize that leadership, titles, and positions of organizational authority are only part of the leadership landscape. Now think of all the relationships in which you have the opportunity to influence the thinking and behavior of others, and consider how often in any given situation you face the choice: "Am I seeking to serve or to be served?" The answer to that question will depend on whom we choose to follow.

That leads to our second key question.

Am I Willing to Follow Jesus As My Leadership Role Model?

You might say, "Before I look to Jesus as my leadership role model, I need to understand what leading like Jesus means." The essence, the core concept of leading like Jesus is encapsulated in the "not so with you" mandate that Jesus gave to His disciples regarding how they were to attain and carry out roles of leadership. In Matthew 20, we read,

> Jesus called them together and said, "You know the rulers of the Gentiles lord it over them, and their high officials exercise authority over them. *Not so with you*. Instead, whoever wants to be great among you must be your servant, and whoever wants to be first must be your slave—just as the Son of Man did not come to be served, but to serve, and to give his life as a ransom for many." (vv. 25–28, emphasis added)

This call by Jesus to servant leadership is clear and unequivocal; his words leave no room for plan B. He placed no restrictions or limitations of time, place, or situation that would allow us to exempt ourselves from His command. For followers of Jesus, servant leadership isn't an option; it's a mandate. Servant leadership is to be a living statement of who we are in Christ, how we treat one another, and how we demonstrate the love of Christ to the whole world. If this sounds like serious business with profound implications—it is!

The exciting part of leading like Jesus is that He never sends us into any situation alone or with a flawed plan or a plan to fail. Jeremiah 29:11–14 tells us,

> "For I know the plans I have for you," declares the LORD, "plans to prosper you and not to harm you, plans to give you hope and a future. Then you will call upon me and come and pray to me, and I will listen to you. You will seek me and find me when you seek me with all your heart. I will be found by you," declares the LORD.

As in all things, when Jesus speaks to us about leadership, He speaks about what is right and effective. We can trust His Word as an expression of His unconditional love and sacrifice for our eternal well-being. As followers of Jesus, we can trust Him regardless of our circumstances, and we can freely ask Him to give us wisdom in all things, including our leadership roles. James 1:2–8 reminds us that Jesus wants to be intimately involved in all aspects of our lives:

> When all kinds of trials and temptations crowd into your lives, my brothers, *don't resent them as intruders, but welcome them as friends!* Realize that they come to test your faith and to produce in you the quality of endurance. But let the process go on until that endurance is fully developed, and you will find you have become men of mature character with the right sort of independence. And *if, in the process, any of you does not know how to meet any particular problem he has only to ask God—who gives generously to all men without making them feel foolish or guilty—and he may be quite sure that the necessary wisdom will be given him.* But he must ask in sincere faith without secret doubts as to whether he really wants God's help or not. The man who trusts God, but with inward reservations, is like a wave of the sea, carried forward by the wind one moment and driven back the next. That sort of man cannot hope to receive anything from God, and the life of a man of divided loyalty will reveal instability at every turn. (PHILLIPS, emphasis added)

A friend of ours once had a counselor who kept reminding him, "Your intelligence has gotten you into this." In other words, in a variety of situations he thought he was smart enough to figure it out on his own. But he wasn't. He was trying to play for the approval of all kinds of audiences, many of whom had conflicting views of what he ought to be doing and how he ought to be living his life. And he ended up pleasing none of them. He had yet to learn that he had but one audience, and that is God. In fact, God is not only the audience of his life, but He is also the director. God will guide and direct us to do exactly the right thing—if only we will let Him.

Is Jesus a Relevant Role Model for Us Today?

A common barrier to embracing Jesus as a leadership role model lies in skepticism about the relevance of His teaching to your specific leadership situations. We are, in many ways, faced with the same questions that Peter faced when Jesus asked him to do some highly unusual and unorthodox things regarding his fishing business.

Here was the situation as described in Luke 5:1–11:

> One day as Jesus was preaching on the shore of the Sea of Galilee, a great crowd pressed in on him to listen to the word of God. He noticed two empty boats at the water's edge, for the fishermen had left them and were washing their nets. Stepping into one of the boats, Jesus asked Simon [Peter], its owner, to push it out into the water. So he sat in the boat and taught the crowds from there. When he had finished speaking, he said to Simon, "Now go out where it is deeper and let down your nets, and you will catch many fish." "Master," Simon replied, "we worked hard all last night and didn't catch a thing! But if you say so, we'll try again." And this time their nets were so full they began to tear! A shout for help brought their partners in the

> other boat and soon both boats were filled with fish and on the verge of sinking. When Simon Peter realized what had happened, he fell to his knees before Jesus and said, "O, Lord, please leave me—I'm too much of a sinner to be around you." For he was awestruck by the size of their catch, as were the others with him. His partners James and John, Zebedee's sons, were also amazed. Jesus replied to Simon, "Don't be afraid! From now on you'll be fishing for people!" And as soon as they landed, they left everything and followed Jesus. (NLT)

What do you think was going through Peter's mind when he replied, "Master, we have been fishing all night and we haven't caught a thing?" It sounds like he might have been thinking something along the lines of this: "I have been listening to Jesus address the crowds with great power and wisdom. I really respect Him as a teacher and for His knowledge of God's Word. But now He has asked me to do something that goes totally against my own knowledge and instincts about how to run my business. He doesn't know fishing. I know fish and fishing; it's my business, and this is not a practical plan. If I do what He says, it is probably going to be a waste of time and energy, and my workers are going to wonder if I have lost my mind."

Peter's skepticism, however, did not prevent him from taking a leap of faith because of who gave him the instructions. Because of his faith, he experienced miraculous results, and he was overwhelmed by what he perceived was too great a gap between himself and what Jesus would require of him.

Jesus sought to calm Peter's doubts and fears and issued an invitation to come and be transformed for a higher purpose. And He is issuing the same call to us. Jesus knows fish. He also knows your business, whether it is in the service of an organization or in a life role.

One way of putting Jesus to the test would be to apply the same criteria to His knowledge, experience, and success that you would to the hiring of a business consultant. Take a few minutes and consider if you would hire Jesus as your leadership consultant in your life role leadership or organizational leadership positions based on His earthly experience.

To help you in this decision-making process, reflect on the following leadership challenges you might be facing, and then ask yourself, "Does Jesus have any relevant practical knowledge or experience in dealing with the following types of leadership issues I face day to day?"

Yes/No

______ Working with or living and caring for imperfect people

______ Taking time to train, develop, and delegate

______ Under constant scrutiny and testing of commitment and integrity

______ Required to handle rejection, criticism, and opposition

______ Facing fierce competition and conflicting demands from friends and foes

______ Tempted by instant gratification, recognition, and misuse of power

______ Facing serious personnel issues, including turnover and betrayal

______ Required to communicate in a multicultural environment

______ The need to challenge the status quo and hierarchy to bring about change

______ The need to communicate a radically new vision of the future

______ The need to call attention to poor leadership at great personal risk

______ The need to put career or relationships on the line to serve a higher purpose

---

Chances are you answered "yes" to every situation. Why? Because Jesus had experience in every situation you face. The book of Hebrews says of Jesus,

> Because he himself suffered when he was tempted, he is able to help those who are being tempted. . . . For we do not have a high priest who is unable to sympathize with our weaknesses. But we have one who has been tempted in every way, just as we are—yet was without sin. Let us then approach the throne of grace with confidence, so that we may receive every mercy and find grace to help us in our time of need. (2:18; 4:15–16)

In addition to His leadership resume, Jesus understood from years of personal experience the challenges of daily life and work. Although Jesus was God, He was not ashamed to do a man's work. He spent the first thirty years of His life on earth as a workingman—the carpenter of Nazareth. We can never sufficiently realize the wonder of the fact that Jesus understands a day's work and knows the difficulty of making ends meet. He knows the frustration of ill-mannered customers and clients who won't pay their bills. He knows the difficulties of living in an ordinary home and in a big family, and He knows the problems that beset us in the everyday world.[1]

Think about how Jesus would do your job differently than you would. As the following scriptures suggest, Jesus wants to do His work in you and through you:

- "Come to me, all you who are weary and burdened, and I will give you rest. Take my yoke upon you and learn from me, for I am gentle and humble in heart, and you will find rest for your souls . . ." (Matthew 11:28–29)
- "I am the vine; you are the branches. If a man remains in me and I in him, he will bear much fruit; apart from me you can do nothing." (John 15:5)
- "If you remain in me and my words remain in you, ask whatever you wish, and it will be given you." (John 15:7)
- "If you love me, you will obey what I command. And I will ask the Father, and he will give you another Counselor to be with you forever—the Spirit of truth. The world cannot accept him, because it neither sees him nor knows him. But you know him, for he lives with you and will be in you. I will not leave you as orphans; I will come to you." (John 14:15–18)

Pause and Reflect

If you are skeptical about adopting Jesus as your leadership role model, write down your reasons. What is it about Jesus that is causing you to doubt? What is it about you that is causing you to hold back?

How Do I Lead Like Jesus?

Even if you've come to the conclusion that you are a leader and that you are willing to follow Jesus as your leadership role model because He has the leadership resume to respond to the issues you face, you are probably asking, "How do I lead like Jesus?"

There are two aspects of leading like Jesus. The first is an understanding that leading like Jesus is a transformational journey. The second and most important, which is the essence of this book, is to learn and internalize the four domains of leadership.

Leading Like Jesus Is a Transformational Journey

Learning to lead like Jesus is more than an announcement; it is a commitment to lead in a different way. This change will not happen overnight. In fact, as the diagram on the following page shows, we believe leading like Jesus is a transformational cycle that begins with personal leadership and then moves to leading others in one-on-one relationships, then to leading a team or group, and finally, to leading an organization or community. We feel this sequence is true in both life role leadership and organizational leadership roles.

During His time on earth, Jesus poured His life into the training of

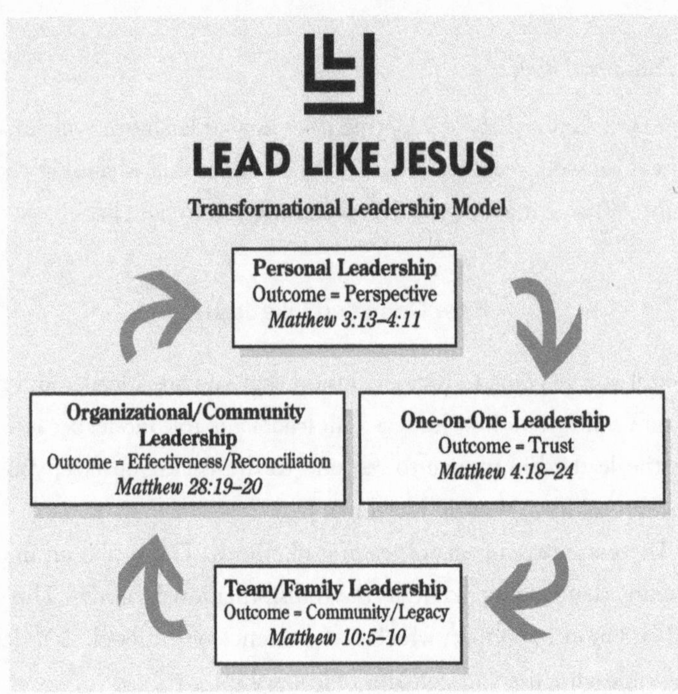

His disciples in the first three leadership arenas: personal leadership, one-on-one leadership, and team leadership. During that process, He equipped them to follow His leadership mandate after He was gone as they moved to the fourth level: organizational leadership.

Personal Leadership

Effective leadership starts on the inside. Before you can hope to lead anyone else, you have to know yourself. We call this personal leadership because it involves choice.

Every leader must answer two critical questions:

1. Whose am I?
2. Who am I?

The first question—"Whose am I?"—deals with choosing the primary authority and audience for your life. In other words, whom are you trying to please? Leaders often demonstrate whose they are by how they define success in today's world. They think success has to do with earthly power and position, as well as performance and the opinions of others.

You can state it any way you like, but Scripture teaches us that ultimately we are created to please God. In the personal leadership arena, you first have to choose whether or not you will please God.

The second question—"Who am I?"—deals with your life purpose. Why did the Lord put you on earth? What does He want to do through you? Scripture teaches that true success is the fulfillment of the life mission God planned for you. Your success in life depends on your relationship with Christ and what level of control you will let Him have in your life. Are you willing to surrender all to Him and to live as He would have you live, rather than how you want to live?

The natural outcome of deciding to please God as well as turning over control of your life to Him is a transformation of your perspective. If you live a life that is not designed to please God or give Him control, your perspective will remain inward and focused on self. If you live your life to please God and put him in charge, your perspective will be transformed to one that is outward and characterized by God-given confidence that will lead your life.

Early in His ministry, Jesus demonstrated His desire to please only the Father and to turn control of His life over to Him. Jesus made His choice public when He surrendered all to His Father and insisted that

John baptize Him "to fulfill all righteousness" (Matthew 3:15). Jesus' desire to please the Father was demonstrated even more dramatically after His baptism, when He went into the wilderness and was tempted by Satan. The events recorded for us in the Gospels show us that during this time Jesus affirmed whose He was and who He was. He determined that He would live by the mission His Father had given Him for the accomplishment of His Father's purpose. In all these situations, Jesus chose the will of His Father.

A great example of transformed personal leadership is the apostle Paul. He was born in Tarsus, a pure Hebrew of the tribe of Benjamin (Philippians 3:5). He was educated as a rabbi and lawyer in Jerusalem under Gamaliel, one of the greatest teachers of the Law of the day (Acts 22:3). So he knew God's Word. He zealously persecuted Christians and pursued them as they fled Jerusalem, even to Damascus, which was 130 miles away.

Then he met Jesus on the road to Damascus (Acts 9:5). During his dramatic encounter with Jesus, Paul was blinded by a light and remained blind for three days until Ananias laid hands on him as the Lord had commanded. Through the power of the Holy Spirit, Paul's sight was restored. He was baptized and then began to declare boldly in the synagogues that Jesus was the Son of God. As a result, his life was threatened (Acts 9:20–25). He went alone into Arabia and after a time returned to Damascus (Galatians 1:15–19). After three years of preaching, Paul finally arrived in Jerusalem, where he met the other disciples, and his ministry to the Gentiles was confirmed.

Clearly, the apostle Paul had the knowledge he needed. He had gone through a long period of preparation. He knew the Word of God. When he finally met Jesus, he made a heart commitment. However, that did not mean he was ready to minister. His initial enthusiasm did not generate the results he hoped for. So he went to Arabia and spent time with God, completing the integration of what he knew in his mind with what he had experienced in his heart.

During his time in Arabia, Paul's personal leadership transformation became complete—he fully surrendered to God and God's plan for him, he began to trust in God's presence and provision, he became confident in God's unconditional love, and he accepted and abided in Jesus. He then returned to Damascus prepared to teach and equip.

A Transformed Personal Lead Like Jesus Perspective

After thinking, writing and teaching about leading like Jesus for several years, Phil began to feel personally disconnected from the message. One afternoon before presenting a Lead Like Jesus Encounter, he sat quietly in his hotel room to see if he could reconnect with what Lead Like Jesus meant to him. The following statements were the result of that time of reflection. It may be of help in framing your own personal perspective.

- I have been called and have accepted the invitation to enter into a special personal relationship with Jesus Christ as my Savior, my Lord, my teacher, and my friend.

- As a follower of Jesus, I enjoy great privilege in personal access to His wisdom and provisions for living in harmony with God's plan and purpose for me as an unceasing spiritual being with an eternal destiny in God's great universe.

- I am the object of God's affection and through the blood of Jesus enjoy an inexhaustible supply of unconditional love, acceptance, and value that is not at risk or dependent on my performance.

- I am a temporary steward of a wide variety of riches on loan from God to be enjoyed, maintained, and used for their intended purpose.
- I will be called to give account for my stewardship when all the things of this world are returned to the owner.
- All those I seek to lead are made in God's image and are the objects of His affection. He calls me to treat them as His special concern.
- By seeking to serve rather than be served as I lead others, I will make Jesus smile.
- Jesus never calls me to follow a flawed plan or a plan to fail, including how I am to lead others.
- I have been called not to success but to obedience as a witness to others and as an active agent of God's plan for His kingdom.
- I accept and find joy in the truth that apart from Jesus I can do nothing, but I can do all things through Christ who strengthens me.

One-on-One Leadership

Once leaders see life with a transformed perspective through self-examination, they are able to develop a trusting relationship with others. Without *trust*, it is impossible for any organization to function effectively. Trust is essential for two people to work together. It is important to note, though, that the outcome of trust will never be achieved or maintained if the first arena of development—personal leadership—has not been addressed. If a leader has a self-serving perspective, people will only move toward him or her for as long as their own self-interests are met.

We can turn to Jesus again as our example of servant-hearted one-on-one leadership. At the beginning of His ministry, after spending time in the wilderness, where His life purpose and perspective were affirmed by trials and temptations, Jesus began the process of calling His disciples. Once they agreed to follow Him, Jesus spent three years building a culture of trust with those men. This trust between Jesus and His disciples would not have developed if Jesus had not first spent time in the wilderness affirming whom He would follow in life and who He was going to be!

In life role relationships, trust is the stream on which vulnerability, caring, commitment, and grace flow between parents and children, husbands and wives, brothers and sisters, friends and fellow citizens. Trust pours first from loving hearts committed to serve and support one another, through promises kept, to encouragement and appreciation expressed, through support and acceptance, to repentance and apologies accepted, to reconciliation and restoration. Yet trust is a stream with a fragile ecological balance: once it is polluted, it will take time and effort to restore.

The always-present power to restore intimacy and broken trust is love. Read the following words from the apostle Paul, and ponder anew the cleansing and healing properties of love:

> If I speak in the tongues of men and of angels, but have not love, I am only a resounding gong or a clanging cymbal. If I have the gift

of prophecy and can fathom all mysteries and all knowledge, and if I have a faith that can move mountains, but have not love, I am nothing. If I give all I possess to the poor and surrender my body to the flames, but have not love, I gain nothing.

Love is patient, love is kind. It does not envy, it does not boast, it is not proud. It is not rude, it is not self-seeking, it is not easily angered, it keeps no record of wrongs. Love does not delight in evil but rejoices with the truth. It always protects, always trusts, always hopes, always perseveres. (1 Corinthians 13:1–7)

Pause and Reflect

- List three ways you nurture trust in your leadership.
- List two things you do that put trust in your leadership at risk.
- Think of a time when you lost trust in a leader. How did you feel? How long did it last? When did you forgive him or her?

Team Leadership

When the ability to develop and sustain trust in one-on-one relationships is applied at the team and family level it produces empowerment and community. Effective leaders working at the team level realize that to be good stewards of the energy and efforts of those committed to work with them, they must honor the power of diversity and acknowledge the power of teamwork. As the saying goes, "None of us is as smart as all of us."

Once again, we look to Jesus as a model for team leadership. After Jesus spent time personally teaching and modeling the type of leadership He wanted them to adopt, He sent out His disciples to minister in teams of two (Mark 6). In doing so, Jesus empowered them to act on His behalf to support one another in accomplishing the work they had been trained to do.

Trust is also a key factor in successful implementation at the team level. Without the trust developed in the one-on-one relationship, empowerment will never happen. Individuals in the group will not empower each other to accomplish an assigned task if they do not trust each other. Failure to empower is one of the key reasons that teams are ineffective.

When it comes to team leadership in the family, things really get interesting. In family leadership, the leader's efforts and aspirations to serve the best interests of others often come in direct conflict with his or her own immediate priorities and demands. The rewards of family leadership are most apt to be found in the subtle fashioning of loving relationships and the slow growth of personal character.

The family leader's example determines how family members treat people of all ages and conditions; how they view success, failure, and adversity; how they solve problems; and how they communicate love and self-worth. If a family leader believes that his self-worth is the result of his performance plus the opinion of others, he is likely to pass on those priorities and values to the next generation by how he treats them. On the other hand, if the family leader demonstrates humility, grace, and an open reliance on God, His Word, and His promises, these traits are likely to flow into the family members.

Sorting out in a family what needs to be done, by whom, when, and for what purpose can be as challenging as any team leadership situation. In family leadership, the language of love will be taxed to express encouragement in the face of colossal, well-meaning failures and messes; patience in times of lost focus, lost keys, and lost phone messages; clear direction and purpose to the reluctant, the annoyed, and the clueless; manners and standards to the rebellious and the doubting; and sympathy and grace to the prodigal and wounded.

The outcome of family leadership is more than the income. The family leader passes on his or her values, priorities, heritage, and identity through behaviors and choices that allow interdependence and loyalty. Family leadership is expressed by the growth, development, and nurture of each member throughout the cycle of life. It is also where external circumstances have the least credibility as an indicator of success.

Coming from circumstances of privilege and opportunity does not guarantee success as God defines it, nor does being raised in circumstances of abuse and poverty consign someone to failure. In any circumstance, at any time, anyone can choose to follow Jesus. In that moment, the external circumstances pale in comparison to the inner resources that knowing and following Jesus provides.

Pause and Reflect

How do you think the people in your family would describe your leadership in the following situations?

- a time of crisis
- a time of failure
- a time of victory
- a time of plenty
- a time of want

Do you like what you would hear? If not, why?

Organizational and Community Leadership

The quality of a leader's influence at a broader organizational or community level depends on the outcome of a transformed perspective, trust, empowerment, and community attained at the first three levels in his or her transformational leadership journey. The outcome of focusing on this level is organizational *effectiveness*, both high performance and high human satisfaction.

It is important to note that when Jesus began His ministry on earth, He did not start at the organizational level. He could have come to the existing organizations of the faithful in His day and said, "OK, gentlemen, I'm here, I'm in charge, and this is the way we will change things!" Instead, Jesus chose to take the approach of a servant leader and quietly influence the lives of a small group of men whom He then trusted and empowered to impact the world.

By valuing both relationships and results, Jesus created the environment for developing an effective organization. In His own life, He was aligned with the purpose His Father had for Him. Jesus also clearly identified the purposes for His followers and their organizations when He gave us the Great Commandment and the Great Commission. But Jesus, in His incarnate form, never implemented the organizational level. He equipped His disciples in the first three levels and then sent the Holy Spirit to guide them at the organizational leadership level, a process that we see developing in the book of Acts.

When organizational leadership enters into the arena of community leadership, it calls for the leader to willingly extend service for the common good. Life role leadership in the community focuses on finding common ground and reconciliation with people of diverse opinions, backgrounds, priorities, and spiritual perspectives. Community leadership requires love to be spoken in truth and courage with good will and tolerance without wandering from moral and ethical conviction.

Jesus spent significant time interacting in positive ways with people who disagreed with Him. He did not isolate Himself from those who disagreed; he embraced those who disagreed. He did not change His message to gain approval, but He continued to love those who did not accept His message.

Community leadership is not restricted or defined by a formal position. It is the willingness to speak out for your values in a manner that recognizes the rights of others and the obligation to honor God in all you do. It means walking the extra mile, turning the other cheek, loving your neighbor, forgiving those who persecute you, and being salt and light.

The various how-tos of leadership in the community include informed, principle-based voting; standing up for what is right over what works; responding with honor when called to serve on juries; praying for all who stand in harm's way on behalf of the community; lending a helping hand to those in need; and seeking to understand those who are different from you.

The consequences of community leadership may come as a test of conviction when challenged or attacked. They may come as a temptation to compromise principle for practicality. They may come in the form of recognition that tempts pride. They call for the leader to answer the questions "Who am I?" and "Whose am I?" again and again and again.

A word of warning: because our life role relationships are based on loyalty and commitment for a lifetime, we can fall into the trap of relying too much on their resilience and our ability to regain lost ground, lost intimacy, and lost love. Life role relationships are worthy of daily renewal and nurture in light of the fact that we never know when and how they will end. As Ken's wife, Margie, often says, "We need to keep our 'I love you's' up to date."

One of the primary mistakes that leaders today make, when called to lead, is spending most of their time and energy trying to improve things at the organizational level before ensuring that they have adequately addressed their own credibility at individual, one-on-one, or team leadership levels.

The Four Domains of Leading Like Jesus

Leading like Jesus involves the alignment of four leadership domains: *heart*, *head*, *hands*, and *habits*. The internal domains—the motivations of your *heart* and the leadership perspectives of your *head*—are things you keep inside or even disguise if it suits your purpose. The external domains—your public leadership behavior, or *hands*, and your *habits* as experienced by others—will determine whether people will follow you.

When your *heart*, *head*, *hands*, and *habits* are aligned, extraordinary levels of loyalty, trust, and productivity will result. When these areas are out of alignment, frustration, mistrust, and diminished long-term productivity will result. We have found that the biblical books of Matthew, Mark, Luke, John, and Acts are filled with rich examples of how Jesus functioned in each of these domains.

Heart

Leadership is first a spiritual matter of the heart. Whenever you have an opportunity or responsibility to influence the thinking and the behavior of others, the first choice you are called to make is whether to be motivated by self-interest or by the benefit of those you are leading. The heart question that Jesus asks is, "Are you a servant leader or a self-serving leader?"

It was clear time after time, whether it was when Jesus gave His "not so with you" instructions to the disciples after John and James's mother requested a special place for her sons in heaven (Matthew 20:20–28) or when Jesus used a towel and a basin to wash the disciples' feet (John 13:3–5), that He modeled leadership as first and foremost an act of service. The subtleties of the heart and the veils of justification we place over self-serving motives require brutal honesty to uncover and put right.

Head

The journey to leading like Jesus starts in the *heart* with motivation. Your intent then travels through another internal domain, the *head*, which examines your beliefs and theories about leading and motivating people. All great leaders have a specific leadership point of view that defines how they see their role and their relationships to those whom they seek to influence. Throughout His season of earthly leadership, Jesus continued to teach and emphasize His point of view, which was servant leadership. As Jesus said in Mark 10:45, "For even I, the Son of Man, came here not to be served but to serve others, and to give my life as a ransom for many" (NLT).

Hands

Others will experience and observe what is in your *heart* and *head* when your motivations and beliefs about leadership affect your actions (*hands*). If you have a servant heart and a servant leadership point of view, you will become a performance coach. That involves setting clear goals and then observing performance, followed by praising progress and redirecting inappropriate behavior.

We believe that if you apply what it means to lead like Jesus to your heart, head, hands, and habits, you will be in a position to radically transform your leadership.

A performance coach realizes that people who produce good results feel good about themselves. Jesus poured Himself into His disciples for three years so that when He left His earthly ministry, they would be able to carry on His vision. The principles of establishing clear goals and measuring performance are common concepts for all types of organizations and apply with equal power to life role leadership relationships. In a family, these principles apply to everything from setting values and behavior guidelines to describing what a clean room looks like to a preoccupied teenager.

Habits

Your *habits* are how you renew your daily commitment as a leader to serve rather than to be served. As a leader committed to serve despite all the pressures, trials, and temptations He faced, how did Jesus replenish His energy and servant perspective? His habits! Through a life pattern of solitude and prayer, knowledge of the will of God expressed in His Holy Word, and the community He shared with a small group of intimate companions, Jesus was constantly refreshed and renewed.

Are You Willing to Lead Like Jesus?

We believe that if you understand that leading like Jesus is a transformational journey and you apply what it means to lead like Jesus to your *heart*, *head*, *hands*, and *habits*, you will be in a position to radically transform your leadership. We are confident in this claim, not because of any brilliance on our part but because of the One you will encounter—Jesus.

As you come to know Him in a new way as the ultimate teacher and model of effective leadership, we hope you will choose to answer His call to "Come, follow me" and learn to lead like Jesus. Are you willing? If not, pass this book on to someone else.

If you want to lead like Jesus, this book will help you discover the leader you already are and the one you can become by learning to lead with your *heart*, *head*, *hands*, and *habits* like the greatest leadership role model of all time—Jesus of Nazareth. These four dimensions of leadership form the outline for the rest of this book. Enjoy, learn, and become a servant leader like Jesus!

Summary

- If you want to lead like Jesus, you have to answer three key questions:
    1. Am I a leader?
    2. Am I willing to follow Jesus as my leadership role model?
    3. How do I lead like Jesus?

- There are two types of leadership: life role leadership and organizational leadership. Everyone is a leader in some part of life.

- The process of transformational leadership moves from personal leadership to one-on-one leadership to team leadership to organizational leadership. This process applies to both life role leadership and organizational leadership positions.

- Leading like Jesus involves the alignment of four leadership domains: *heart*, *head*, *hands*, and *habits*.

Chapter 2

THE HEART OF A SERVANT LEADER

Most leadership books and seminars focus on the leader's behavior and try to improve leadership style and methods. Emphasis is on the *hands* of the leader. They attempt to change leadership from the outside. Yet in teaching people to lead like Jesus, we have found that effective leadership starts on the inside; it is a *heart* issue. We believe if we don't get the heart right, then we simply won't ever become servant leaders like Jesus.

The most persistent barrier to leading like Jesus is a heart motivated by self-interest.

In one sense, we all enter this world with self-focus. Is anyone more self-centered than a baby? A baby doesn't come home from the hospital asking, "How can I help around the house?" As any parent can attest, all children are naturally selfish; they have to be taught how to share. A mature adult realizes that life is about what you give rather than what you get.

In Philippians 2:1–4, the apostle Paul urges us to look out for others' interests, not just our own. He says,

> If you have any encouragement from being united with Christ, if any comfort from his love, if any fellowship with the Spirit, if any tenderness and compassion, then make my joy complete by being like-minded, having the same love, being one in spirit and purpose. Do nothing out of selfish ambition or vain conceit, but in humility consider others better than yourselves. Each of you should look not only to your own interests, but also to the interests of others.

A heart motivated by self-interest looks at the world as a "give a little, take a lot" proposition. People with hearts motivated by self-interest put their own agenda, safety, status, and gratification ahead of that of those affected by their thoughts and actions. Cutting people off on the freeway or the church parking lot, punishing those who disagree with you or challenge your position, and exploiting the weaknesses and fears of others to get what you want are all actions that come from a self-motivated heart.

Your Heart's EGO—Edging God Out or Exalting God Only?

As you consider the *heart* issues of leadership, a primary question you have to ask yourself is, "Am I a servant leader or a self-serving leader?" The fact is that we all fall short of perfection and give in to the temptation to behave as self-serving leaders in certain situations. This question,

A heart motivated by self-interest looks at the world as a "give a little, take a lot" proposition. People with hearts motivated by self-interest put their own agenda, safety, status, and gratification ahead of that of those affected by their thoughts and actions.

when answered with brutal honesty, reveals your motivation as a leader. It also reflects your heart's EGO: do you seek to Edge God Out or to Exalt God Only in the way you exert influence on those around you? The answer to that question reveals whether you are driven to protect and promote yourself or called to a higher purpose of service.

Pause and Reflect

In which of the following situations am I most prone to put my own agenda ahead of those I lead:

____ in my work

____ in my home

____ in my marriage

____ as a volunteer

Why do you think this happens?

Early in our Leadership Encounters, we came to realize that we all sometimes Edge God Out in the self-serving way we seek to influence others. Few leaders would admit to being self-serving, yet we observe self-serving leaders all the time. Self-serving leaders say, "Given the choice, I'll make a decision that benefits me." If these leaders are working in an organization, all the money, recognition, power, and status move up the hierarchy toward them. If they are in a family, they treat their children and spouses as supporting cast members in their quest to fulfill their personal agenda and self-image.

What makes people self-serving? In his classic book *Ordering Your Private World*, Gordon McDonald identifies a helpful distinction. He says there are two types of people in the world: *driven* people and *called* people.[1]

Driven people think they own everything. They own their relationships, they own their possessions, and they own their positions. In fact, they perceive their identity as the sum of their relationships, possessions, and positions. As a result, driven people spend most of their time protecting what they own. We see this in a family when a parent makes sure everyone knows that he is the father (or she is the mother) and demands that everyone else cater to his wishes without questioning his authority. *Driven* people think and act as if "he who dies with the most toys wins." And if you mess with any of their toys, you're in trouble. The possessions of driven people become an important expression of who they are and end up possessing them.

Called people, on the other hand, believe everything is on loan. They believe their relationships are on loan; they know that we have no guarantee we will see those we love tomorrow. Called people also believe their possessions are on loan and are to be held lightly, to be enjoyed and shared with an open hand. Finally, called people believe their positions are on loan from God and the people they are attempting to influence. Rather than protecting what they own, called leaders act as good stewards of what has been loaned to them.

Are You a Self-Serving Leader or a Servant Leader?

Three distinctive patterns of behavior mark the difference between self-serving leaders and servant leaders: how you handle feedback, how you handle successor planning, and your perspective of who you think leads and who follows.

How Do You Handle Feedback?

Self-serving leaders spend most of their time protecting or promoting the things in which they have invested their self-worth and security, such as their public image, their reputation, their competitive performance, their position, their possessions, or their personal fulfillment in their intimate relationships. Whenever they sense a threat to the things they cherish, they are likely to react in a fearful, defensive way. This is especially true when they receive negative feedback. They think negative feedback means people don't want them to lead anymore. That is their worst nightmare! The biggest fear of self-serving leaders is not failure; it is the fear of losing their power and position—the very things in which they have placed their self-worth and security.

Because servant leaders believe their position and influence are on loan to those whom they serve, they are more prone to see feedback as a gift rather than a threat. Even when feedback may be hurtful or given in a negative way, a servant leader grounded in God's unconditional love can get beyond initial negative emotions and seek to find any truth and value for improving their leadership. After all, their position is on loan to their people.

Pause and Reflect

Which of the following words best describes your usual reaction to negative feedback?

____ Fear

____ Anger

____ Denial

____ Sadness

____ Curiosity

____ Gratitude

If you could alter your response, which attitude to feedback would be most productive for you and the people you lead?

How Do You Plan for Successors?

"Well done, good and faithful servant" (Matthew 25:21). In those few words, Jesus summed up what we would all like to hear when final judgment is rendered for our efforts to make a difference in the world around us. One aspect of a job well done as a servant leader is how well we have prepared others to carry on after our season of leadership influence is completed. Our leadership legacy is not just limited to what we accomplished, but it includes what we leave behind in the hearts and minds of those with whom we had a chance to teach and work.

Perhaps you haven't thought of your leadership position or relationship as a season. But if you reflect on your experience, you probably can see that you have had several seasons of leadership influence with your family, your career, or your volunteer activity. Your personal succession planning efforts speak volumes about your motives as a leader. It is unlikely that anyone leading from an EGO involved in the promotion and protection of self—Edging God Out—is going to spend much time training and developing their potential successor. Just as avoiding honest feedback is a mark of an EGO-driven leader, so is failure to develop someone to take your place.

During His time on earth, Jesus modeled sacrificial passion for ensuring that His followers were equipped to carry on the movement. He lived His legacy in intimate relationship with those He empowered by His words and example. In his book *Transforming Leadership*, Leighton Ford notes, "Long before modern managers, Jesus was busy preparing people for the future. He wasn't aiming to pick a crown prince, but to create a successor generation. When the time came for Him to leave, He did not put in a crash program of leadership development—the curriculum had been taught for three years in a living classroom."[2]

A good way to gauge your progress in leading like Jesus is to ask yourself the following questions: "How well am I doing in preparing others to take my place when the time comes? Do I consider them a threat or an investment in the future? Am I willing to share what I know and provide opportunities to learn and grow for those who will come after me? If not, why not?" A few moments of brutal honesty regarding your motives as a leader are worth years of self-deception.

Jesus modeled the heart of a true servant leader by investing most of His ministry time training and equipping the disciples for leadership. Near the end of His earthly ministry, Jesus told His disciples, "I no longer call you servants, because a servant does not know his master's business. Instead I call you friends, for everything I learned from my Father, I have made known to you" (John 15:15). He also said to His disciples—and to us, "I tell you the truth, anyone who has faith in me will do what I have been doing. He will do even greater things than these because I am going to the Father" (John 14:12).

Pause and Reflect

Do you view training your successor or the next generation as a threat, a burden, or an opportunity to extend your leadership impact beyond your season of influence? How does your successor planning impact your daily, weekly, quarterly, or yearly priorities?

Who Leads and Who Follows?

The term *leader* is mentioned only six times in the King James Version of the Bible, while the term *servant* is mentioned more than nine hundred times. That fact highlights the third distinction between a self-serving leader and a servant leader: who leads and who follows? Self-serving leaders think they should lead and others should follow. Servant leaders, on the other hand, seek to respect the wishes of those who have entrusted them with a season of influence and responsibility.

Throughout His life and leadership, Jesus affirmed that God is not looking for leaders but for servants who will let Him be the Leader and who will focus first on the kingdom of God. When God came to Abraham, God had the plan and Abraham was instructed to carry it out according to God's promise. When God came to Moses, God provided leadership for the shy, retiring man. When God came to Mary, she surrendered to God's will and undertook the role of servant leader with her infant son. When God came to Paul, God had a plan that this passionate man spent the rest of his life fulfilling through his leadership and witness to the Gentiles. When God was the leader and these faithful people were servants, His plan was effectively accomplished.

On the other hand, whenever we become the leader and try to make God the servant, things don't work out. Why? Because our EGO gets in the way, and we Edge God Out! If you want your life to be significant, then you have to recognize that it's all about God, not about you. As the old Yiddish saying goes, "If you want to make God laugh, tell Him your plans."

If, as a leader, you want to follow the mandate Jesus gave us—to serve rather than to be served—you have to realize that every day you will face all kinds of challenges to your good intentions. Our adversary consistently tries to get us to be self-serving. To resist the temptation to be drawn off course, we must understand the dynamics of a self-serving EGO that Edges God Out. This is the biggest heart issue we face in becoming servant leaders.

Edging God Out

We have all been in the presence of and have sometimes even imitated someone who is at least temporarily obsessed with his or her own self-importance. Self-important leaders fill the air with "I," "my," and "me" statements as they enumerate their trials, triumphs, and opinions. They are highly sensitive to any criticism or any effort to wrench the spotlight and the microphone from their hands. If there is any credit to be taken for a success or for being right on any subject, they are the first and the last to speak on the subject. What on the surface looks like prideful self-promotion is probably an expression of a more basic sense of at-risk self-esteem and security.

Without God-grounded confidence, we set up elaborate defenses to protect our always-at-risk sense of security and self-worth. We hide behind the rights and privileges of our position, hoard control, revenue, and information, and keep others at a safe distance. This leaves us vulnerable to making the wrong decisions for the wrong reasons and diminishing the value of our influence and trust.

How do we Edge God Out as individuals and as leaders? If we want to learn to lead like Jesus, we have to overcome several barriers. The following diagram illustrates the ways the heart of a self-serving leader Edges God Out:

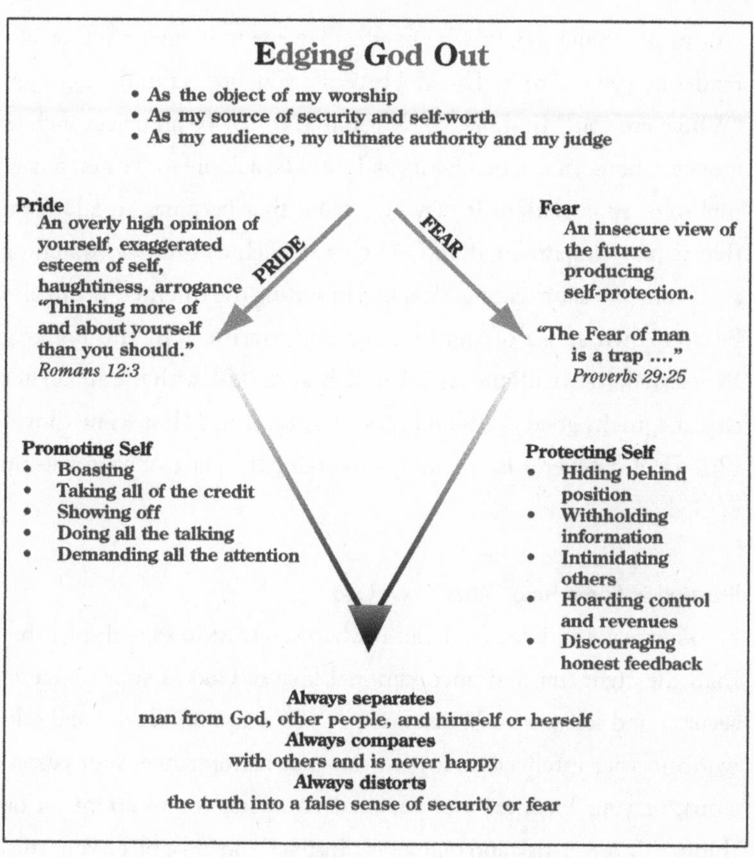

You can Edge God Out as the only One worthy of your worship; your source of security and self-worth; and your only audience, authority, and judge.

Putting Something in God's Place

First, you Edge God Out when you put something else in God's place as the object of your worship. Whenever anything becomes more important to you than God, you are in effect bowing to it, adoring it, or surrendering yourself to it. The idol becomes your answer to the question "Whose are you?" In short, you worship it. It may be an object such as money, a house, a car, or a business. It may be a desire for power, recognition, or appreciation. It may be a habit that becomes an addiction that is more important than God to you, such as exercise, watching sports on television, eating, sleeping, or surfing the Internet. It can also be your own sense of significance and sacrifice. In the book of Revelation, Jesus calls the church at Ephesus to task with the complaint that despite its good deeds and perseverance, it had "lost its first love" (2:1–7). Whatever it is, it's not worth taking the place of your worship of God.

Trusting in Something Other Than God

Another way you Edge God Out is when you trust in something other than the character and unconditional love of God as your source of security and self-worth. When you put your sense of security and self-worth in your intellect, your position, your performance, your possessions, or your business and personal contacts, you're counting on things that are at-risk and temporary. Instead, you must place your trust in that which is sure and eternal: God's care for you and the wisdom He provides about living in harmony with the rest of His creation.

Valuing Opinions Other Than God's

A third way you Edge God Out is when you put others in His place as the major audience, authority, and judge of your life. If your sense of security is based on what others think, then you don't have any security at all. People are fickle, and your ability to please everyone all the time is a myth that leads to anxious trying and no peace of mind or soul. Not only is God the all-knowing, all-seeing audience of your life, He has the eternal power and unconditional love to reconcile all things according to His pure and perfect wisdom.

All the world is a stage, and God is the all-seeing audience. He determines your destiny. How many business and church leaders thought they were getting away with devious deals and decisions only to discover that God makes known from the housetops the secrets that were whispered in the closet? Your character is revealed when no one is watching. (Except remember that God is always watching!)

EGO Problems—Pride and Fear

Edging God Out as the One we worship, as our source of self-worth and security, and as our primary audience results in two kinds of EGO problems: pride and fear. When false pride and toxic fear enter into a relationship, they poison it. When they become the driving force in our leadership decisions, they render them ineffective.

Self-serving leaders react to things that happen to them. If you say something to them or do something that hooks their pride or fear, they *react*. They spend little time considering what is in the best interests of others or their relationships. They shoot from the hip and sometimes end up shooting themselves in the foot. Pride or fear-filled people are quick to judge, quick to take offense, quick to speak, and quick to push blame away and pull praise closer.

Servant leaders, on the other hand, *respond* to things that happen to them. Before taking action, they are able to step back, even for a second or two, from the emotion of the moment and apply some value checks to the situation out of a desire to serve the common good. They are quick to listen, slow to judge, slow to anger, and quick to turn the praise light onto someone else.

Pride

Pride centers on the promotion of self. It is, as we read in Romans 12:3, thinking of yourself "more highly than you ought." Here are some of the ways you can tell that pride is at its destructive work. See if any of these seem familiar:

- When you are engaged in a discussion, you resist acknowledging that the other person's idea is actually better than your own. In other words, "The righter they sound, the madder you get."
- You start to do all the talking, taking too much credit, demanding all the attention, boasting, showing off, or demanding service on the basis of your position.
- You judge the value of an idea by who said it rather than by the quality of the thought.
- You treat people as too far below you in position or credentials to seek out their input on issues that affect them.
- Your image becomes more important than substance and truth.
- You act as if the rules, judgments, and standards you impose on others should not apply to you because of who you are or the position you hold.
- Your compensation becomes more important as a mark of success than the ethical and relational price you paid to attain it.

- Winning and losing become the only criteria you value and character becomes an option.
- You look in the mirror to find the source of all success and out the window for the cause of failure.

Pause and Reflect

Acting out of pride is like trying to blow up a balloon with a hole in it. It is lonely business requiring consistent effort with only temporary results that never satisfy or please anyone. Think of a time when you blew up a balloon and there was a hole in it, and you will have a good mental image of what happens when you put your self-esteem in your performance and the opinion of others.

The Bible has much to say on the subject of pride. Proverbs 13:10 tells us, "Pride only breeds quarrels." Proverbs 16:18 says, "Pride goes before destruction and a haughty spirit before a fall." And Proverbs 16:5 declares, "The LORD detests all the proud of heart. Be sure they will not go unpunished."

Some people reading these words will say, "But that's not me. I don't have any false pride. I know that everything comes from God and is on loan to me." That's great. But often there is a more subtle way in which we Edge God Out—fear!

Fear

The other dynamic of Edging God Out is fear. Most people don't normally recognize fear as an EGO issue, but it is at the root of many seemingly prideful behaviors.

The capacity to fear is a gift from God. When applied as intended, fear can keep us focused on doing the right thing for the right reasons. Yet what we actually do with the gift of our capacity to fear often prevents us from enjoying its benefits. Instead of enhancing life as a dimension of keeping our focus on God, fear has poisoned human relationships ever since man first stepped out of God's will. The first thing Adam and Eve did after they ate the forbidden fruit was become self-conscious, cover up, and hide in fear. In a way we have been hiding ever since, in fear that our weaknesses and bad behavior will be found out. The irony is that God—the only one who matters on an eternal scale—already sees and knows it all.

The temptation to toxic fear is something we all face every day. It is a dark force that can color our relationships and permeate our souls. As Usman Asif said, "Fear is the darkroom where negatives develop." Fear is a complete anti-God state of mind. It is a good thing turned bad.

In both the Old and New Testaments, the fear of God and fear of man are placed at the extremes of good and evil. We are called to hold God in life-giving, reverent awe as the ultimate source and judge of our self-worth and security. Life-giving fear is, as W. E. Vine defines it, "wholesome dread"—a heartfelt desire not to dishonor or grieve the One who has extended His compassion, mercy, and grace to us.[3] Being agitated by fear into fight-or-flight thinking and behavior is life threatening in the most personal and profound way.

In Psalm 111:10, we read, "The fear of the LORD is the beginning of wisdom"; and in Proverbs 14:26, we read, "He who fears the LORD has a secure fortress, and for his children it will be a refuge." God as the preeminent object of wholesome fear is made clear at the end of Ecclesiastes by King Solomon, who gives the definitive statement of the positive purpose and application of our capacity to fear: "Now all has been heard; here is the conclusion of the matter: Fear God and keep his commandments, for this is the whole duty of man" (12:13).

In stark contrast to the wholesome awe of God, Proverbs 29:25 tells us, "Fear of man will prove to be a snare." Jesus poses the core question regarding the right use of the gift of fear when He tells His followers: "I tell you my friends, do not be afraid of those who can kill the body and after that can do no more. But I will show you whom you should fear: Fear him who, after the killing of the body, has the power to throw you into hell. Yes I tell you, fear him" (Luke 12:4–5).

If fear or awe of God is appropriate and necessary in our faith, then how do we avoid the toxic fear of man? We have to understand the root cause of toxic fear. What is its common denominator? The answer lies in our addictive dependence on at-risk sources of security and self-worth. A good, workable definition of *addiction* is "an ever-increasing desire for something that has an ever-decreasing ability to satisfy." Addictions, both positive and negative, start as a voluntary attempt or choice to experience something desirable and end up as a compulsion that grows continually stronger and out of control. When we seek safety from pain and loss of self-esteem in at-risk things like our possessions and our positions, we are vulnerable to anxiety and fear as key drivers for our thoughts and behaviors.

When we feel that our source of supply for the things we are addicted to is at risk, toxic fear can poison our daily decisions and relationships in a wide variety of ways. Here are some examples:

- Rob is a workaholic who is afraid to slow down and look at the condition of his life. He feels trapped when his wife or kids ask for help or when forced into a period of inactivity due to illness. He keeps up a schedule of late hours and early mornings to avoid the gnawing feeling of emptiness.

- Janet is a control freak who is afraid of failure, so she chooses personal exhaustion rather than training others and delegating to them. By micromanaging and keeping other people dependent on her for information, she seeks to protect herself from becoming obsolete or losing her source of power.
- Craig is a fitness addict who goes into an emotional and relational tailspin at the first sign of illness or his own aging or the aging or illness of someone with whom he is identified.
- Cynthia is an approval addict who fears rejection and broods over a 2 percent negative rating on a feedback form or an overheard piece of unfavorable gossip.
- Tracy is a teenage relationship junkie who will do bad things with bad people rather than face being alone.

Each of these examples of toxic fear is a variation on a central theme. To borrow the title from an old song, each of the people described above is "looking for love in all the wrong places." They have bought into what Robert S. McGee describes as Satan's formula for self-worth. In his classic book *The Search for Significance*, McGee notes, "If Satan had a formula for self-worth he would love you to buy into, it would be Self-Worth = Performance + the Opinion of Others."[4]

Yet our performance is not great all the time, and people are fickle; you can't count on their approval. When we seek to build a secure sense of self-worth on the shifting sands of personal performance and the ever-changing opinions of others, we end up tossed about in a sea of self-doubt and anxiety.

Pause and Reflect

Think of a time when fear of rejection or failure prevented you from doing or saying something that might have helped a friend avoid an impending mistake. What excuse did you give yourself to justify letting your fears control your inaction? Was it worth it?

The Results of Pride and Fear

It is interesting to see how false pride, fear, or self-doubt play out in organizational leaders. When leaders are addicted to any of these ego afflictions, their effectiveness erodes dramatically. Leaders dominated by false pride are often called controllers. Even when they don't know what they are doing, they have a high need for power and control. Even when it's clear to everyone that they are wrong, they keep on insisting they are right. They don't want someone to look like they know what they are doing for fear others might think those people should be managing instead of them. That is why they seldom support their people. If everyone is upbeat and confident, the controller throws out the wet blanket. They support their bosses more than their people because they want to climb the hierarchy and be part of the bosses' crowd.

At the other end of the spectrum are the do-nothing bosses who are often described as "never around," "always avoiding conflict," and "not very helpful." Plagued by fear and self-doubt, these leaders often leave people alone even when those people are insecure and don't know what they are doing. Do-nothing bosses don't seem to believe in themselves or trust in their own judgment. They overvalue others' thoughts—especially the thoughts of those they report to—more than their own. As a result, they rarely speak out and support their own people. Under pressure, they defer to whoever has the most power.

If any of this sounds a bit too close for comfort, don't be alarmed. Most of us have traces of both false pride and self-doubt because the issue is really the EGO. We Edge God Out as our primary focus, and as a result, we are stuck, all alone, focusing only on ourselves.

The three primary results of Edging God Out through pride and fear are separation, comparison, and distortion of the truth. Let's look at each of these results.

Separation

Pride and fear always separate us from God, from each other, and us from ourselves. Here are some common examples of the separating power of pride and fear:

Separation from God

- Too ashamed about failure to talk to God
- Too arrogant to pray
- Too afraid of the answer to ask God the question
- Too full of our own agenda to wait for God to reveal His agenda

Separation from other people

- Too prideful to say we need help or we don't understand
- Too fearful of rejection to take a stand

- Too fearful to say no when no is the right answer
- Too fearful of losing control to share information or power
- Too convinced of our own opinion to consider conflicting information

Separation from ourselves

- Too sensitive to others' opinions to listen to our own heart
- Too busy fixing others' problems to look at the mess inside
- Too much making excuses and too little repenting
- Too full of our own agenda to wait for God

One of the greatest challenges in seeking to lead like Jesus is the intimacy it requires. The biggest barrier to intimacy is a fear of vulnerability—fear of having to admit you don't know all the answers, that you may need help, and that your abilities as a leader may be in question. Here false pride is fear in action.

When we lose intimacy with God and His unconditional love, we fear intimacy with others. Like the wizard behind the curtain in Oz, we hide behind intimidating false fronts and place barriers around ourselves rather than expose our own inadequacies and needs. The isolation created by the fear of intimacy leaves leaders vulnerable to being blindsided by changing times and circumstances.

When fear of intimacy enters into a relationship or organization, it acts like a virus. When fear enters through the heart and actions of the leader, it is particularly nasty and hard to cure.

Comparison

The second negative result of addictions to self-pride and fear is that they result in unhealthy horizontal comparisons. Instead of measuring success in terms of how well you are following God's plan for your life, you are constantly tempted to look around to see how you compare with others on a material basis.

The need to compare and draw comfort from comparisons to others is a sign of false pride, insecurity, and fear of inadequacy. Seeking to learn from others and aspiring to emulate good role models are signs of a healthy state of humility in mind and heart. However, the EGO issues and toxic impact of envy, jealousy, or low self-esteem have been polluting human relationships ever since Cain slew Abel. When leaders foster internal competition and rivalries as a way of driving performance, they can erode both performance and relationships.

"A little friendly competition" rarely stays little or friendly when the leader makes the rewards for winning too great and the price of failure too high. When you seek to determine your level of self-worth and security by comparison with others, the end result is either complacency or anxiety. In a larger sense, it devalues the promises and provisions of God, who has already guaranteed your value and security based on His unconditional love. You are His beloved.

Distortion

The third result of addiction to false pride and fear is distortion of the truth. The root cause of toxic fear is a life built on a lie that tells us we are not safe playing things God's way and we are going to miss out on something good. It is FEAR—False Evidence Appearing Real. When pride and fear isolate you from everyone else, including God, your view

The root cause of toxic fear is a life built on

a lie that tells us we are not safe

playing things God's way and we are going

to miss out on something good.

It is FEAR—

False

Evidence

Appearing

Real

of reality will become increasingly misguided and your decisions will be more prone to error.

One of the key distortions that affect leader effectiveness is an EGO-driven fixation on short-term results at the expense of long-term integrity. In today's business world, increased speed and access to information brings with it a demand for quicker decisions and quicker positive results. Tolerance for setbacks or loss of positive momentum in the marketplace grows shorter and shorter. Annual reports are ancient history; real-time data streams and analysis are making quarterly estimates and weekly performance metrics obsolete. Expectations and anxiety built on instant access to data can turn everything into a crisis or a conscience-numbing exhilarating fix for an EGO-addicted leader. You think you have to be on duty 24-7 and report your progress immediately.

Jesus spoke of the perils of distortion borne out of a false sense of security and self-worth that comes about when we Edge God Out. He said,

> Do not store up for yourselves treasure on earth, where moth and rust destroy and thieves break in and steal. But store up for yourselves treasures in heaven, where moth and rust do not destroy, and where thieves do not break in and steal. For where your treasure is, there your heart will be also. (Matthew 6:19–21)

EGO-driven distortion is also manifested in an overblown view of your ability or desire to control events. When you think and act as if everything depends on you, you're setting yourself, and those who follow you, up for failure in the long run. The truth is that each of us works within our limitations as fallible human beings. Factors beyond our control and even our awareness determine success and failure. This does not diminish the importance and value of your efforts, but it puts them in a perspective that will allow grace and humility to flow in your relationships and leadership.

Now that you understand how our heart's EGO Edges God Out and often blocks our intention to serve rather than be served, we will examine the antidote to this phenomenon—Exalting God Only.

Exalting God Only

The mirror image of Edging God Out is Exalting God Only. The key to this transformation is altaring your leadership EGO. *Altaring* is not misspelled. That's exactly what you have to do—put your EGO on the altar and Exalt God Only, as the diagram on the following page illustrates.

Worship God Only

If we are to lead like Jesus, then we need to worship like Jesus. Worship is a heart issue. All the forms of worship are empty if our heart isn't in them. In the Bible, people worshiped when they saw God or some evidence of God's presence, power, or worth. So worship starts with God and ends with God. We respond to His initiative.

Worship means to bow down or to serve. Worship is an act of reverence and has the root idea of trembling or fear—being in awe of God.

Depend on God Completely

To Exalt God Only, we must worship Him above all, rely on Him as the source of our self-esteem and security, and honor Him as the omniscient audience and authority for our decisions. Jesus is the supreme

Exalting God Only

- As the object of my worship
- As the source of my security and self-worth
- As the omniscient audience and judge of my life decisions

Humility

- Something lived but never claimed
- Looking out the window rather than in the mirror to praise
- A Kingdom perspective of cause and effect

Confidence

- Resting assured in God's nature, goodness, purpose, plan, process, and provision
- Transparency and effectiveness
- Proceeding in faith one step at a time

Community and Fellowship
Contentment and Generosity
Trust and Truth
Inspiration and Commitment

How to Altar My Leadership EGO

- Embrace an eternal perspective of the *here and now* in light of the *then and there*
- Seek to lead for a higher purpose
  - Beyond success
  - Beyond significance
  - To obedience and surrendered service
- Scrupulously assess my level of trust and surrender to what I believe about God, His Kingdom, and His claim on my life and leadership
- Seek the promised guidance of the Holy Spirit, the ultimate Coach

example of this second emphasis of depending on God the Father as His source for everything—including self-esteem and security. He said,

> The Son can do nothing by himself; he can do only what he sees his Father doing, because whatever the Father does the Son also does. For the Father loves the Son and shows him all he does. Yes, to your amazement he will show him even greater things than these. . . . By myself I can do nothing; I judge only as I hear, and my judgment is just, for I seek not to please myself but him who sent me. (John 5:19–20, 30)

Exalt God as Your Only Audience and Judge

True worship means that your eyes are on God and not on others. He is your audience of One; everyone else is in the cast. Jesus was scathing in His judgment of the scribes and Pharisees, whom He called hypocrites because they did their good deeds to be seen by men: "Everything they do is done for men to see . . . they love the place of honor at banquets and the most important seats in the synagogues; they love to be greeted in the marketplaces and to have men call them 'Rabbi'" (Matthew 23:5–7).

Don't do your acts of worship for people. Instead, Jesus said acts of worship are to be done in secret for Him to see rather than made a public show.

Be Aware That God Is Watching You

Our tendency is to be aware only of people who watch us. When you recognize that God is your audience and judge, it affects everything you do. All of life becomes a worship experience if you are always aware of God's presence and do everything to His glory.

Benefits of Exalting God Only—Humility and Confidence

If God is the object of our worship, the source of our security and self-worth, and our only audience and authority, false pride and fear are replaced by humility and God-grounded confidence. Instead of being driven by pride and fear when we Edge God Out, our relationships and leadership will be renewed with humility and God-grounded confidence when we seek to Exalt God Only. The challenge is to understand the nature of the journey we must travel and then commit to taking the first steps.

Humility

Leading like Jesus means leading with humility, which requires knowing whose you are and who you are. You are called to be a good steward of your season of influence in service to a plan that was set in motion before you came on the scene. Your influence will extend beyond your exit in the hearts and minds of those entrusted to your care. It means seeing yourself not "more highly than you ought, but rather [thinking] of yourself with sober judgment, in accordance with the measure of faith God has given you" (Romans 12:3).

As a leadership trait, humility is a heart attitude that reflects a keen understanding of your limitations to accomplish something on your own. It gives credit to forces other than your own knowledge or effort when a victory is won or an obstacle overcome. According to Jim Collins in his book *Good to Great*, a leader with a humble heart looks out the window to find and applaud the true causes of success and in the mirror to find and accept responsibility for failure.[5] A leader who does that is not coming from low self-esteem. In fact, people with humility don't think less of themselves; they just think of themselves less.

Leading like Jesus requires humbly receiving and honoring the non-negotiable boundaries He has set for accomplishing true and lasting results. Jesus said to His disciples, "I am the vine; you are the branches. If a man remains in me and I in him, he will bear much fruit; apart from me you can do nothing" (John 15:5).

There is a difference between putting on the appearance of humility before others and being truly humble in the presence and purposes of God. You are not to be piously humble about what He has given you or what you have done. Fred Smith, in his book *You and Your Network*, says it well: "People with humility don't deny their power; they just recognize it passes through them, not from them."[6]

One of Ken's first leadership lessons occurred when he came home after school excited about having just been elected president of his seventh-grade class. His dad was a career navy man highly decorated for his leadership efforts in the South Pacific during World War II. When Ken told his dad the great news of his election, his dad said, "Son, it is great that you have been elected president. But now that you have that position, don't ever use it as a way of getting others to do what you want. The best use of power is not to have to use it at all. People follow great leaders because they respect them, not because they have power." That was quite a lesson for an emerging leader.

The humility that Jesus demonstrated did not arise from lack of self-esteem, love, power, or ability. His humility came from the fact that He knew who He was, where He came from, where He was going, and whose He was. That permitted Him to treat people with love and respect.

Humility is realizing and emphasizing the importance of others. It is not putting yourself down; it is lifting others up. It is saying to yourself and others, "I am precious in God's sight—and so are you!"

Confidence

Humility born out of a secure and obedient relationship with His Father allowed Jesus to approach every situation with God-grounded confidence, the second attribute of a heart that Exalts God Only. Jesus always knew He was unconditionally loved by His Father. That gave Him confidence to stay focused on the reason He had come.

Norman Vincent Peale often said the toughest test of self-esteem is bowing your head, admitting to God that you fall short of perfection, and accepting Jesus as your Savior. Some people would tell him, "Christianity is for sissies." Norman would laugh and say, "That's furthest from the truth. The human ego does not want to admit any weakness." Moving from self-confidence to God-grounded confidence takes a big person and an even bigger, loving God.

One of the by-products of God-grounded confidence is the "peace of God, which transcends all understanding" (Philippians 4:7). Jesus promises to give us this peace when we surrender our lives to Him: "Peace I leave with you; my peace I give to you. I do not give to you as the world gives. Do not let your hearts be troubled and do not be afraid" (John 14:27).

What a blessing it is to live each day knowing that through Jesus, we have access to a peace with God that is beyond our ability to understand. Our peace and confidence do not depend on our performance. Bringing God into any day is just a prayer away. We can rejoice in amazing grace that lifts us up and supports us and comes only from God.

Pause and Reflect

How long has it been since you have felt truly at peace?

Are you willing to make some changes in how you treat others?

Altaring Your Leadership EGO

To successfully combat the temptation to be self-serving in your leadership, every day you must put your EGO on the altar and Exalt God Only.

The antidote to the temptations of instant gratification, recognition, and power that plague all leaders is the Cross. Leaders must not only ask, "What would Jesus do?" but they must also remember what He did and what He promises. Hebrews 12:1–3 gives us the secret to avoiding a life that Edges God Out:

> Therefore, since we have so great a cloud of witnesses surrounding us [those who persevered in faith against great temptation and great trials], let us lay aside every encumbrance and the sin that so easily entangles us, and let us run with endurance the race that is set before us, fixing our eyes on Jesus , the author and perfecter of faith, who for the joy set before Him endured the cross, despising the shame, and has sat down at the right hand of the throne of God. For consider Him who has endured such hostility by sinners against Himself, so that you may not grow weary and lose heart. (NASB)

Changing Your Perspective

When we altar our leadership EGO and begin to Exalt God Only, our perspective changes. Edging God Out separates us from God, from others, and from ourselves; compares us with others; and distorts the truth into a false sense of security. When we Exalt God Only, we move toward community and transparent relationships rather than separation and isolation, from comparison to contentment with who we are and whose we are, and from distorting the truth to seeking the truth as a basis of decision making.

Pause and Reflect

The first step to wellness is admitting you have an EGO problem beyond your control that is worth fixing. Ask yourself this: Do you Edge God Out more out of fear or out of pride? What evidence is there? Examine your inner thoughts, and evaluate how much your false pride and your fears dominate your relationships. What is your first reaction when somebody criticizes you or disagrees with your decision? Do you become defensive? What is your first reaction when you fail at something or make a mistake? Do you think about covering up because you're worried about what people will think of you if they find out? When faced with unexpected change, is your first thought, "How is this going to affect me?" rather than, "How will this affect those who look to me for leadership?"

With a little brutal honesty, you will probably come to realize that you, too, have an EGO problem. That's the bad news. The good news is that you are not alone and that what you are struggling with is a treatable condition. In 1 Corinthians 10:13, we read,

> No temptation has seized you except what is common to man. And God is faithful; he will not let you be tempted beyond what you can bear. But when you are tempted, he will also provide a way out so that you can stand up under it.

This applies to letting your pride and fear control your thoughts and actions as a leader.

EGO Anonymous—Taking the First Step to Exalting God Only

Since we feel that Edging God Out is the biggest addiction of all, we hold EGO Anonymous (EA) meetings in our Leadership Encounters to help people get in touch with the powerful, negative impact that false pride and fear can have on their relationships and leadership.

We always start our EA meetings by saying, "All EA meetings are voluntary. If your ego has never gotten in your way through false pride (promoting your self-interest) or though fear (protecting your self-interest), then you can leave." More than ten thousand people have participated in EA meetings during the last few years, and no one has ever left.

To give you a sense of how an EGO Anonymous meeting works, we are going to let you sit in on one as an observer. In a real EA meeting, there are no observers—only people who are actively trying to work on their ego addiction. The people you will meet are fictitious, but the issues they raise come from real people involved in real-life leadership situations.

Welcome to EGO Anonymous

"Hi, my name is Michael, and I am an EGO maniac," said the man standing in front of his folding chair. "Hi, Michael," the group replied with a tone of acceptance. The man continued, "Since our last meeting, my pride impacted my leadership at home when it kept me from admitting to myself and to my wife that she was right about a lousy investment choice I had made. Instead of owning my mistake, I got mad at her for being right. It took me too long to apologize." As Michael sat down, the group applauded and several of the men in the group nodded in understanding.

Next to stand was a well-dressed businesswoman on the other side of the circle. "Hi, my name is Laura," she said in a tone that indicated that she was used to speaking in public. "Hi, Laura," the group responded.

"I am an EGO maniac," Laura continued. "As the president of a large advertising firm, my pride gets in the way when I become impatient with the people who work for me. Last week, I took back an assignment I had delegated to one of my key new team members and did the work myself. I ended up overloaded, and she ended up demoralized." The usual applause followed as Laura resumed her seat.

Silence followed, as often happens at an EGO Anonymous meeting until someone else is motivated to share how his EGO has sabotaged his efforts to be an effective leader. After about a minute, a tall, gray-haired man with a thoughtful face rose slowly. "Hi, my name is Steven," he said in a quiet voice. The group reached out again: "Hi, Steven."

"I am an EGO maniac," Steven said. "My ego takes the form of fear of success. I am the pastor of a rapidly growing church, and I am reluctant to give my approval for expansion. I am afraid I won't be able to handle any more demands on my time and energy." His humble admission of self-limitation was met with healing applause that signaled understanding.

In contrast to the quiet demeanor of the pastor, the next person to stand was an athletic-looking man in his midthirties whose quick movements and energetic style radiated intensity. "Hi, my name is Darnell." The group responded, "Hi, Darnell."

"I am an EGO maniac," Darnell replied in an almost aggressive manner. "As a high school basketball coach, my ego impacts my leadership when my desire to win and my fear of failure cause me to make choices that are not always in the best interest of the growth and development of my players." The group clapped as the openness and honesty of Darnell's statement sunk in.

The tentative, almost apologetic manner of the next person to stand was in sharp contrast to the coach's high energy. "Hi, my name is Karen," said the attractive, casually dressed young woman. The group responded warmly, "Hi, Karen."

"I am an EGO maniac," she continued. "As the mother of two small children, my ego gets in the way when my low self-esteem and fear of inadequacy makes me feel like a victim and robs me and my kids of any joy that we could share." The group nodded in understanding.

Next, a middle-aged man with a salt-and-pepper beard stood and said, "My name is Rich." The group encouraged him with their greeting: "Hi, Rich."

"Up until today I would have said that I was not an ego maniac. I really don't have any pride. I know that everything I have comes from God. But today, I've discovered that I am an EGO maniac. I've Edged God Out because of my fear. There are so many things I know He's wanted me to do, and I either haven't attempted them or I've settled for less than I clearly knew He wanted." The group applauded his confession to demonstrate their support and understanding.

The pattern of reflective silence and the sharing of personal triumphs and failures in dealing with the twin demons of pride and fear continued for another twenty minutes until everyone who wanted to had the opportunity to share his or her story.

Pause and Reflect

Imagine you were the next person to stand up at this EA meeting. How would you describe the EGO problem that has the biggest impact on how you lead people?

The Twelve Steps of EGO Anonymous

The meeting we described dealt with the first step of a Lead Like Jesus twelve-step program we have developed for leaders who want to bring new hope and effectiveness into their lives and relationships by leading like Jesus. The full twelve-step program, adapted from Alcoholics Anonymous (AA),[1] is as follows:

1. I admit that on more than one occasion I have allowed my EGO needs and drive for earthly success to negatively impact my role as a leader and that my leadership has not been the servant leadership that Jesus modeled.
2. I've come to believe that God can transform my leadership motives, thoughts, and actions into the servant leadership that Jesus modeled.
3. I've made a decision to turn my leadership efforts over to God and to become a disciple of Jesus and the servant leadership He modeled.
4. I've made a searching and fearless inventory of my own leadership motives, thoughts, and behaviors that are inconsistent with servant leadership.
5. I've admitted to God and at least one other person the exact

nature of my leadership gaps—when I behave in ways that do not make Jesus proud.

6. I am entirely ready to have God remove all character defects that have created gaps in my leadership.
7. I humbly ask God to remove my shortcomings and to strengthen me against the temptations of recognition, power, greed, and fear.
8. I've made a list of those people whom I may have harmed by my EGO-driven leadership and am willing to make amends to them all.
9. I've made direct amends to such people whenever possible unless doing so would injure them or others.
10. I continue to take personal inventory regarding my leadership role, and when I am wrong, I promptly and specifically admit it.
11. By engaging in the disciplines of solitude, prayer, study of Scripture, and belief in God's unconditional love for me, I seek to align my servant leadership effort with what Jesus modeled and to constantly seek ways to be a servant first and a leader second with the people I encounter in my leadership responsibilities.
12. Having had a "heart attack" regarding the principles of servant leadership, I have tried to carry this message to other leaders and practice them in all my affairs.

While the first step of admitting your addiction is all-important, completing all twelve steps is necessary for people to make a complete journey of overcoming their addiction to Edging God Out.

Lead Like Jesus Through Forgiveness and Grace

One of the results of altaring your leadership EGO from Edging God Out to Exalting God Only is taking on the perspective of the here and now in light of the then and there. In other words, it means developing a way of looking at your daily leadership choices with eternity in mind. What you focus on will determine what view of the future you serve.

Self-serving leaders go about in a never-ending pursuit of short-term pleasure fixes for their material-based self-esteem. In doing so, they use people as a means to an end and justify it by whatever incidental benefits trickle downhill to the followers as a positive result of their self-serving leadership.

Leading like Jesus calls for a radically different perspective and priority—seeking first the kingdom of God. In the Sermon on the Mount, Jesus set forth the priorities for all who would be His followers: "Seek first [God's] kingdom and his righteousness, and all these things [the necessities of life] will be given to you as well" (Matthew 6:33).

What does seeking first the kingdom of God mean in terms of our leadership decisions? It means bringing an eternal perspective into the realm of practical, day-to-day leadership decisions that effects better results and better relationships. It means revising the way we see people, situations, and priorities to the way God sees them, and inviting the Holy Spirit into our relationships to infuse into our thoughts and actions two key elements of leading like Jesus—forgiveness and grace.

The Way of Forgiveness

Why is forgiveness important as an aspect of leadership? Because forgiveness is how servant leaders respond to mistakes and errors. And forgiveness is the way for a heart grounded in the unconditional love of God to respond to the imperfections of others.

Jesus established the centrality of forgiveness in His leadership when He cried out from the cross, "Father, forgive them, for they do not know what they are doing" (Luke 23:34). One of the most frequent tests of whether we have the heart attitude required to lead like Jesus is how we deal with the failures of those we lead to perform according to plan. Remember, getting things roughly right is simply part of the learning process that precedes getting things exactly right on a consistent basis.

Leaders, seeking to grow and develop people as an end goal of equal importance to results, need a healthy capacity to forgive, correct, and move on. EGO-driven leaders, impatient for results, are quick to judge and discount less-than-perfect efforts as failure rather than to forgive and redirect.

Forgiveness is a supernatural act, not a natural response to being hurt or let down. It is an act of the will of one who has surrendered control to a higher court of judgment. Forgiveness is a hallmark of what it means to lead like Jesus. He taught forgiveness to His disciples, He practiced it with those who betrayed Him, and He granted it willingly to those who participated in His death on the cross.

As leaders, the journey of forgiveness must start with us. Unlike Jesus, we all fall short of 100 percent in our journey as leaders. Sometimes we make mistakes that could have been avoided. Sometimes we say or do things in the heat of the moment that we regret. If our EGO is wrapped up in our performance and the opinion of others, we will be unable to forgive our own shortcomings, let alone anyone else's.

Let's look, for just a minute, at what Scripture says about this. Romans 14:13 says, "Forget about deciding what's right for each other.

Here's what you need to be concerned about: that you don't get in the way of someone else, making life more difficult than it already is" (MSG). And in James 4:11 we find, "Do not speak evil of one another, brethren. He who speaks evil of a brother and judges his brother, speaks evil of the law and judges the law. But if you judge the law, you are not a doer of the law but a judge" (NKJV).

The opposite of forgiveness is judgment. Your motivation for doing something is as important as what you do. In theological terms, judgment is pointing out a fault with a view to condemnation. On the other hand, discernment is pointing out a fault with a view to correction or restoration. When we withhold forgiveness, is it because we are sincerely trying to correct or restore—or is it because there is some benefit to us in condemning?

Forgiveness is a particular dimension of an even broader element of the leadership of Jesus—grace.

Pause and Reflect

The price of forgiveness is letting go of the right to require either payment or an apology for a wrongdoing. Whom do you need to forgive in order to restore a relationship with someone who let you down?

The Way of Grace

"Grace is the currency of all true relationships." This insightful statement was made by Father Joseph Fox, O. P., who worked as the director of personnel in the Vatican. When he shared this statement with us, it was like a light bulb going on. We realized that the key to a leader ministering to followers inflicted with false pride or fear, as well as followers witnessing to leaders inflicted by the same, is the power of grace.

Grace extends unrestrained fellowship to others in celebration of their inherent dignity as being made in God's image and as the objects of His affection. Grace is at work in relationships when we are present for one another, accepting our mutual limitations and willing to exchange mutual efforts to enhance one another's well-being. It is only in intimacy that grace abounds.

God has reached out in the most profound way to restore our intimate relationship with Him. Even when we walk away from Him in our sin, His grace abounds in that "while we were still sinners, Christ died for us" (Romans 5:8). During His season of leadership, Jesus constantly reached out in unrestrained fellowship and acceptance to heal and restore people to relationships of grace and acceptance. To lead like Jesus, we must come to understand the spiritual dynamics of our relationships as both leaders and followers so that we may be agents of grace in a like manner.

As we have emphasized in this chapter, the issues of the *heart* are keys to leading like Jesus. We are now ready to move to the second internal domain—*the head*. If serving others is central to your heart, then that intention will influence your leadership point of view.

Summary

- As you consider the *heart* issues of leadership, a primary question you have to ask yourself is, "Am I a servant leader or a self-serving leader?"
- Three distinctive patterns of behavior mark the difference between self-serving leaders and servant leaders:

1. How do you handle feedback?
2. How do you plan for successors?
3. Whom do you follow?

- The heart of a self-serving leader Edges God Out by putting something in God's place, trusting something other than God, and valuing opinions other than God's.
- Edging God Out results in two kinds of EGO problems—false pride and fear, which cause separation, comparison, and distortion of the truth.
- The mirror image of Edging God Out is Exalting God Only, which requires altaring your leadership EGO.
- If you are to lead like Jesus, you must worship God only, depend on God completely, exalt God as your only audience, authority, and judge, and be aware that God is watching you.
- When you altar your leadership EGO and Exalt God Only, false pride and fear are replaced by humility and God-grounded confidence.
- When you lead like Jesus, the Holy Spirit extends into your relationships two key elements of leading like Jesus—forgiveness and grace.

Chapter 3

THE HEAD OF A SERVANT LEADER

The journey of servant leadership starts in the *heart* with motivation and intent. Then it must travel through the *head*, which is the leader's belief system and perspective on the role of the leader. All great leaders have a specific leadership point of view[1] that defines how they see their role and their relationships to those they seek to influence and are willing to teach it to others. Jesus' leadership point of view proclaimed that leadership was first an act of service. He spent three years teaching His leadership point of view to His disciples.

Some people think servant leadership means the leader is trying to please everyone or "the inmates are running the prison." Yet that was not what Jesus meant by servant leadership! Did Jesus try to please everyone? When He washed the feet of the disciples and sent them out as His ambassadors, was He commissioning them to do anything the people wanted?

Of course, the answer to both questions is no. Jesus was completely focused on pleasing His Father as His audience of One. That meant proclaiming the gospel and bringing salvation to mankind. He sent His disciples to help people understand the good news and live according to the values of God's kingdom, not just do whatever they wanted. Jesus made it very clear that what He was asking His followers to do, in His name, would not please everyone. He told them up front that they would be subject to all kinds of resistance and persecution for telling people what they did not want to hear.

The Two Roles of Servant Leadership

Skeptics of servant leadership contend that the words *servant* and *leader* don't go together. How can you lead *and* serve? People who think that way don't understand that there are two parts to the servant leadership that Jesus exemplified:

1. A visionary role—setting the course and the destination
2. An implementation role—doing things right with a focus on serving

Some people think leadership is about vision while management is about implementation. When such a distinction is made, management seems to get a second-class status when compared to leadership. We prefer *not* to distinguish between the two, and as a result, we consider both roles as servant leadership roles.

Our point of view is that vision and implementation are two sides of the same coin—each equally important. To maximize results for everyone concerned, we must *lead* by setting course and direction, and then we "flip the coin" and *serve* by empowering and supporting others in implementation.

Leadership is about going somewhere. Effective leadership begins with a clear vision, whether for your personal life, your family, or an organization. If your followers don't know where you are going and where you are trying to take them, they will have a hard time getting excited about the journey. It is especially important to have a compelling vision that provides direction and focuses everyone's energy on getting where they are headed.

According to Ken and Jesse Stoner in their book, *Full Steam Ahead: The Power of Vision,*[1] a compelling vision has three parts.[2] To engage the hearts and minds of others, you must be able to communicate the following three things:

1. *Your purpose.* What "business" are you in? Where are you going and why? Or in terms of your family, what is your family all about? Where is your family going and why?
2. *Your picture of the future.* What will your future look like if you are accomplishing your purpose?
3. *Your values.* What do you stand for? On what principles will you make your ongoing decisions?

A compelling vision tells people who they are, where they are going, and what will guide their journey.

Creating a Compelling Vision

Your Purpose

What business are you in? What are you trying to accomplish? What is your mission statement? Jesus was clear about what business He and His disciples were in. He called His disciples, not just to become fishermen, but to a greater purpose—to become "fishers of men" (Matthew 4:19).

An effective mission statement should express a higher purpose for the greatest good that gives meaning to the efforts of each individual involved in your organization. When Walt Disney started his theme parks, he knew how to excite people. He said, "We are in the happiness business—we make magic!" Wouldn't you rather be in the happiness business than the theme park business? Being in the happiness business drives everything Disney's cast members (employees) do with their guests (customers).

Even if an organization states its mission, if that statement does not support a higher purpose, it will not motivate people. For instance, one congregation said they wanted to be a twenty-four-hour-a-day church. They had a nice facility, and they wanted to keep the rooms busy. But attendance went down because the mission wasn't something the people got excited about. Your purpose needs to inspire people.

At another church, the purpose is more inspiring to the congregation. At the beginning of every service, the minister says, "We believe that a close encounter with Jesus of Nazareth can transform lives. Our mission is to make Jesus smile." Backing up that statement are clear operating and theological values. Attendance has gone up. It's a place where a community comes together with the main purpose of making Jesus smile.

A clear purpose sets the direction for where you are going. At the Lead Like Jesus ministry, our purpose is "to inspire and equip people to Lead Like Jesus to restore joy to work and family." As we have continually emphasized, without clear direction, leadership doesn't matter.

In *Alice in Wonderland*, Alice learned this lesson when she came to a fork in the road. She asked the Cheshire cat which way she should go. When he asked where she was going, Alice replied that she didn't know. The cat concluded matter-of-factly, "Then it doesn't matter which way you go."

Ken's father retired early as a captain in the U.S. Navy. When Ken asked why he left the service early, his dad replied, "I hate to admit it, but I liked the wartime navy a lot better than the peacetime one. Not that I like to fight, but in wartime we knew why we were there and what our purpose was. We knew what we were trying to accomplish. The problem with the peacetime navy is that since nobody knows what we are supposed to be doing, too many leaders think their full-time job is making other people feel unimportant." When you run an organization without a clear purpose, leadership becomes self-focused.

If your organization does not have a mission statement, if your mission statement is not stated so that everyone understands it, or if people are not excited about your mission statement, your organization or family will begin to lose its way. As the Bible says, "Where there is no revelation, the people cast off restraint" (Proverbs 29:18). In other words, without guidance from God, law and order disappear. Without vision, the people perish.

Your Picture of the Future

The second element of a compelling vision is your picture of the future. What will the future look like if things are running as you planned?

Jesus outlined His vision for His disciples when He charged them, "Therefore go and make disciples of all nations, baptizing them in the name of the Father and of the Son and of the Holy Spirit, and teaching them to obey everything I have commanded you. And surely I am with you always, to the very end of the age" (Matthew 28:19–20). That was His picture of the future.

At the Lead Like Jesus ministry, our picture of the future is a Lead Like Jesus movement where someday, everywhere, everyone will know someone who truly leads like Jesus. To accomplish that, we envision the following:

1. Jesus is adopted as the role model for all leaders.
2. All people are being drawn to Jesus by the positive impact of Christians leading like Jesus.

Your picture of the future is what you would like to happen if you live according to your purpose and everything goes well. Do you have a clear picture of the future? What does a good job look like? What will the future look like if things are running as planned? Providing vivid answers to these questions is important both to your people and to your organization.

The view of the future is what keeps people going when times are tough. It will prevent the organization from stopping short or arriving at the wrong destination. In your view of the future, it is important to distinguish between *goals* and *vision*. A *goal* is a specific event that, once achieved, becomes a piece of history to be superceded by a new goal. A *vision*, or view of the future, is an ongoing, evolving, hopeful look into the future that stirs the hearts and minds of people who know they will never see its end or limit.

President John F. Kennedy challenged the American people with the *goal* to put a man on the moon and return him home safely by the end of the decade. When the moon landing was accomplished, NASA lost its purpose until it established a new goal.

Dr. Martin Luther King Jr. challenged America to a *vision* in his "I

A vision, or view of the future,

is an ongoing, evolving, hopeful look

into the future that stirs the hearts and

minds of people who know they will

never see its end or limit.

have a dream" speech. He painted a verbal picture of a spiritually transformed nation, and more than forty years after his assassination, Dr. King's vision continues to stir passion and commitment. Walt Disney's vision, or picture of the future, for his theme parks was that guests would have the same smile on their face leaving one of their parks as they had six, eight, or ten hours earlier when they arrived. Being in the happiness business, that made sense!

Throughout His ministry, Jesus spoke of what His kingdom looked like. He continually talked about the kingdom of God—its values, teachings, parables, miracles, and final fulfillment. He gave the disciples a clear picture of the future, and they committed themselves to that future.

Your Values

The third element of a compelling vision is values—what will govern how you behave in your organization. Values are the nonnegotiable principles that define character in a leader. Fewer than 10 percent of organizations around the world have clear, written values. But values are important because they drive the behavior of people who work on your purpose and picture of the future.

Most companies that have stated values either have too many values or do not have rank-ordered values. Research shows that if you really want to impact behavior, you can't emphasize more than three or four values, because people can't focus on more than those.

Why is it important to state and prioritize your values? Because life is about value conflicts! When these conflicts arise, people need to know what values they should focus on. Without guidelines, people will create their own order of priority, and that may lead away from fulfilling the desired organizational purpose and picture of the future.

As we develop our own value priorities, it is important to know and understand what Jesus set before us as His nonnegotiable priorities. When the Pharisees sought to test Jesus with the question,

> "Teacher, which is the greatest commandment in the Law?" Jesus replied, "Love the Lord your God with all your heart and with all your soul and with all your mind. This is the first and greatest commandment. And the second is like it: 'Love your neighbor as yourself.' All the Law and the Prophets hang on these two commandments." (Matthew 22:36–40)

Notice that Jesus rank-ordered two values:

1. Love God with all your heart, soul, and mind.
2. Love your neighbor as yourself.

Even if they are rank-ordered, values will not drive the accomplishment of a purpose or picture of the future unless they are translated into behaviors. That's what Jesus did throughout his three-year public ministry. Clarifying how values are lived out in behavioral terms allows for accountability and measurement of progress.

Walt Disney seemed to sense both value concerns when he prioritized and rank-ordered his organization's four operating values: safety, courtesy, the show, and efficiency. Most people, when they think about Disney, put courtesy as the number one value, followed by efficiency, because they think that making money would be next in importance. Then they usually put safety third and the show fourth.

Actually, Disney's first priority is safety. "Ahead of courtesy?" you ask. Yes. Walt Disney knew that he must put safety ahead of courtesy, the show, and efficiency, because if guests left the park on a stretcher, they would not have the same smile on their faces leaving the park as they had when entering the park. When you reflect on the fact that they are in the happiness business, that rings true!

Therefore, if a cast member hears a scream while being courteous to a guest, to follow Disney's values, he will excuse himself immediately and focus on the number one value—safety. If these values were not rank-ordered, a cast member enjoying interacting with a guest, upon hearing a scream, might say, "They are always yelling in the park" and then continue talking to the guest. A manager might confront the cast member by saying, "You were closest to the scream; why didn't you react?" The cast member could respond, "I was being courteous."

Why is it important to know that efficiency—running a profitable, well-run organization—is the fourth-ranked value? First of all, it indicates that efficiency is a value. But second, because it is ranked fourth, if Disney employees are following their company's values, they will do nothing to save money if it compromises safety, friendliness, or the show. These are all higher-ranked values.

At the Lead Like Jesus ministry, our rank-ordered values are:

1. Honor God in everything we do.
2. Build relationships based on trust and respect.
3. Maintain integrity and excellence in programs and services.
4. Practice responsible stewardship.

Each of these values is operationally defined. For example, we will know that we are *honoring God in everything we do* when we:

- Give God all the credit.
- Relinquish all problems to His care.
- Seek His face through worshiping together, studying together, and praying together.
- Love one another as He loves us by being a loving truth-teller, honoring each other's commitment, encouraging each other's health and well-being.
- Proceed boldly in living the gospel.

True success in servant leadership depends on how clearly the values are defined, ordered, and lived by the leader.

Everyone is watching. If the leaders live their values, then others are ready to follow suit. Jesus lived His values of love of God and love of His neighbor all the way to the Cross: "Greater love has no one than this, that he lay down his life for his friends" (John 15:13).

Pause and Reflect

Imagine you were being interviewed by your ten-year-old daughter, and she asked you the following question: "What are the four most important rules in our family?" What would your answer be?

Making Tough Value Choices

Many of us will be or already are working in organizations that have established a set of operating values, either intentionally or by default. Conflicts between organizational values and personal values are a reality of life. What do you do when the values of the organization do not align with your own? You may realize this over time as you experience ongoing gaps between established purpose and values and what is acted out on a day-to-day basis. You are faced with a choice: you can compromise your values, seek to be an active influence for change in the organization, or leave.

Leading like Jesus does not include letting the organization change or compromise your values. The core of the temptation to compromise your values is likely to stem from EGO issues—particularly toxic fears, such as fear of rejection, fear of poverty, fear of ridicule, fear of confrontation, or fear of lost position. Jesus dealt with this dynamic of choice when He spoke of the impossibility of serving two masters as the same time: "No servant can serve two masters. Either he will hate the one and love the other, or he will be devoted to the one and despise the other. You cannot serve both God and Money" (Luke 16:13).

Jesus posed the ultimate challenge by spelling out the long-range price of compromise: "What good is it for a man to gain the whole world, and yet lose or forfeit his very self?" (Luke 9:25) He also told us that we can trust in His promise never to leave us alone or outside the range of His care and concern for us.

Leading like Jesus does include the possibility of making a choice to be an agent of change or to seek a more compatible environment. The appropriate response for your circumstances will depend on what God has in mind for you.

Phil Hodges recounts a story from his own experience of having to decide whether to stay or leave an organization where he was experiencing a major values conflict with his boss.

As the senior human resources manager for a large manufacturing operation, I had become increasingly troubled by the atmosphere of fear and dishonesty that was being generated by my boss, who headed up the operation. Although my boss never treated me in a disrespectful manner, he regularly beat up on people who either brought him unfavorable news or didn't perform at his level of expectation.

Regrettably, my boss's personal insecurities and unhealthy perfectionism worked their way into the soul of the organization, creating fear and a look-good-at-any-price mentality. Morale and ethics were at an all-time low. During this same period, I had the opportunity to take advantage of an early retirement package that would have resulted in my leaving the company several years earlier than I had planned. Because of the frustration and embarrassment I felt regarding the state of human resources in this organization, I decided to leave. I went through all the preliminary steps of signing the necessary paperwork and pursued some interesting new career opportunities in teaching and consulting.

Despite all of this, I was not at peace about whether to stay or leave. I had often prayed on the subject but had received no immediate answer. On the Friday morning of the last day for turning in my retirement papers, I was still waiting on the Lord when I began my morning run around the neighborhood. I determined that I would not go back into the house until God showed me what He wanted me to do.

I finished my regular two-mile route and found myself at the front door still without an answer. So I started running a series of two-hundred-yard laps in the street in front of my house while the neighbors were driving to work. During the second lap, I started to think of some scriptures, mostly about Paul and his perseverance under trial, which eventually led me to believe that I should stay rather than leave my job. When I went to work and let the filing deadline pass, I had a great sense of peace about staying put, although the situation did not look promising.

The following Tuesday morning, my boss returned from a business trip to headquarters, walked into my office, closed the door, and proceeded to tell me that he had been removed from his job, effective immediately. When he told me who his replacement was to be, I called some friends back East to find out something about him. The feedback I received was all positive. "An HR man's dream." "Highly ethical." "Poised professional." "A very devout Christian." God is good!

During the next three years, I was blessed to participate in a remarkable turnaround in the ethical and value environment of an organization, based primarily on the leadership of a true servant leader. The things I learned have been invaluable as a basis to helping others learn to lead like Jesus.

For me, the decision to stay and be part of the change was the result of trying to be open to what God had planned. What your experience will be, I don't know. But I can encourage you to wait upon the Lord.

Life and leadership are all about choices. Choices are made based on your values, whether you admit it or not. You are a monument to the choices you have made over the course of your life. If you want to change your life, embrace the values of Christ, the servant leader. What do you stand for?

Establishing Goals

As a leader, once your vision is set, you can then establish goals to answer the question: what do you want people to focus on now? A compelling vision gives goals real meaning.

Like values, people should not have more than three or four main goals. We believe in the 80/20 rule, which says 80 percent of the performance you want from people will come from 20 percent of what they could focus on. So set goals for the 20 percent who will give you the 80 percent.

An important part of goal setting is making sure what good behavior looks like. Anyone who has attempted to get a teenager to clean up his or her room will recognize the cause of frustration that comes when you go back two hours after giving a general instruction—"Clean up your room!"—and the child is standing proudly in the middle of a four-foot-square clean zone surrounded by undisturbed chaos, claiming proudly to have done what you told him to do.

Sometimes, in the haste of the moment, leaders conclude for the sake of personal convenience that they have been "perfectly clear" in their initial instructions about what they want, and then they hold their listeners accountable for perfect comprehension and perfect retention. Serving people well as a leader means testing for understanding and repetition, repetition, repetition. Great leaders almost become like third-grade teachers. They communicate their vision, values, and goals over and over and over again, until people get them right!

Who Is Responsible for the Visionary Role?

What's your purpose? What is your preferred picture of the future? What are your values? If you can't answer those questions, you don't have a clear vision. Without a clear vision, the rest of your leadership skill and effort won't matter. As a leader, if you cut people loose without any direction or guidelines, they will lose their way, and the organization will suffer immeasurably. Guidelines are boundaries that channel energy in a certain direction. It's like a river. If you take away the banks, it wouldn't be a river anymore; it would be large puddle, devoid of momentum and direction. What keeps the river flowing are its banks.

The traditional pyramid hierarchy is effective for this first role of leadership—the visionary/direction role. People look to the leader for vision and direction. As the diagram below suggests, while the leader may involve experienced people in shaping direction, the ultimate *responsibility* for establishing a compelling vision remains with the leader and cannot be delegated to others. Once the vision is set, the rest of organization is expected to be *responsive* to the vision—that is, to live according to its guidelines.

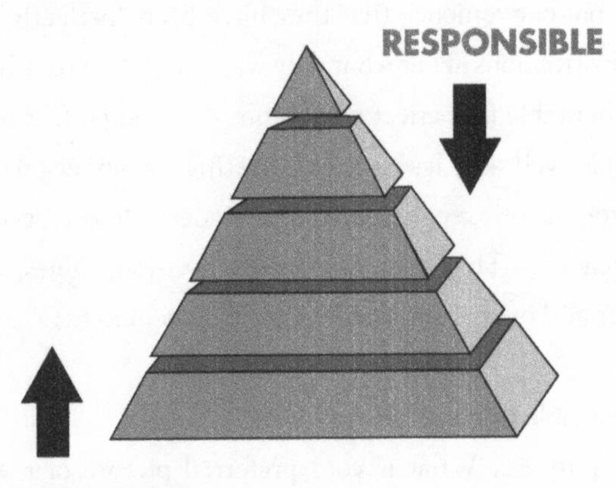

Implementing Your Vision and Goals

Once people have a picture of where you want to take them and why, the leadership emphasis switches to the second role of leadership—implementation. The leader now becomes, in a sense, a servant of the vision, by serving the people who are being asked to act according to the vision and accomplish the goals.

When that occurs, the traditional pyramid hierarchy must be turned upside down so the frontline people who are closest to the customers are at the top, where they can be *responsible*—able to respond—to their customers. In this scenario, leaders serve and are responsive to the needs of their people, training and developing them to soar like eagles so they can accomplish established goals and live according to the vision they have of the customer experience.

In an organization, if a leader does not respond to the needs and desires of his people, these folks will not take good care of their customers. But when the frontline customer-contact people are treated as responsible owners of the vision, they can soar like eagles and create raving fans of their customers rather than quack like ducks.

As the diagram on page 100 suggests, when your frontline people are empowered to take care of the customers, the role of the designated leader moves to the bottom of the hierarchy, where leadership becomes an act of service.

When Jesus washed the feet of His disciples, He was, in a sense, transitioning His focus from the visionary role of servant leadership to the implementation role. As He did that, He, in a sense, turned the pyramid upside down. In the process, He demonstrated the true essence of servant leadership and challenged His disciples to do the same.

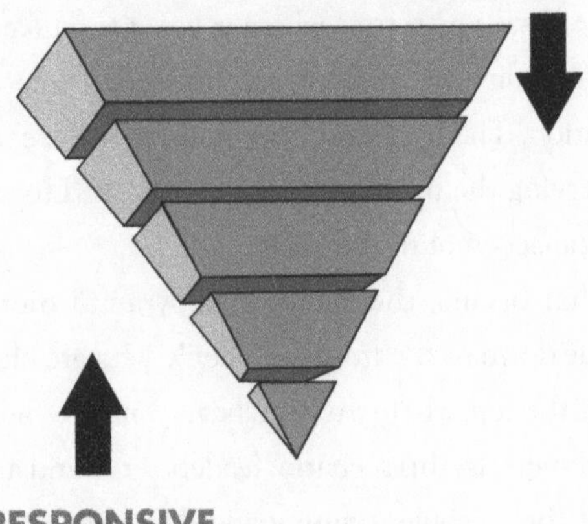

When Jesus had washed the disciples' feet and then put on His robe, He reclined again and said to them,

> Do you understand what I have done for you? You call me "Teacher" and "Lord," and rightly so, for this is what I am. Now that I, your Lord and Teacher, have washed your feet, you also should wash one another's feet. I have set you an example that you should do as I have done for you. (John 13:12–15)

Pause and Reflect

Imagine what an experience that must have been for the disciples as their Lord and Teacher humbled Himself and performed such a personal and intimate service. The image of Jesus washing the feet of the disciples is powerful and humbling. What images come to mind from your own life of someone you know performing an act of humble servant leadership? For example, think about a mother with a newborn child.

While Jesus demonstrated the ultimate in servant leadership, He didn't send His disciples out to serve without clear direction. He did not imply that they should go out and help people do anything they wanted. The vision was clear. He got it from the top of the hierarchy—His Father. As "fishers of men," the disciples were to "go and make disciples of all nations," focusing first on loving God and then on loving their neighbors (Matthew 4:19; 28:19; 22:37–40). And when it came to implementing this vision, Jesus wanted the disciples to be servant leaders who helped others understand and believe the good news.

The implementation role of effective leadership is where most leaders and organizations get in trouble. The traditional hierarchical pyramid is kept alive and well so that all the energy is moving away from the customers, up the hierarchy, because people feel they must please their bosses, leaving the customers neglected at the bottom of the hierarchy.

This happens in a lot of organizations. In this environment, as we have said earlier, self-serving leaders assume that the sheep are there for the benefit of the shepherds. Jesus was talking against this authoritarian hierarchy when He said, "Not so with you" (Matthew 20:26).

If you don't turn the pyramid upside down in implementation, you end up with a duck pond. When there is conflict between what the customer wants and what the boss wants, the boss wins. You have people responding to customers like ducks: *Quack, quack.* "It's our policy." (*Quack, quack.*) "Don't blame me; I just work here." (*Quack, quack.*) "Would you like to speak to my supervisor?" (*Quack, quack.*)

Ken had a personal example of the different experiences you can have with organizations depending on whether they are duck ponds or they permit people to soar like eagles.

> A while before 9/11, I was heading to the airport for a trip that was taking me to four different cities during the week. As I approached the airport, I realized that I had forgotten my license and did not have my passport with me, either. Not having time to go back home and get in to make my flight, I had to be creative because, at that time, there were few, if any, options for identification besides your driver's license and passport.
>
> Only one of my books has my picture on the cover, and that is *Everyone's a Coach*, which I wrote with Don Shula. So when I got to the airport, I ran to a bookstore; luckily, they had a copy of my book. Fortunately, the first airline I had to go to was Southwest Airlines. As I was checking my bag at the curb, the porter asked to see my identification. I said, "I feel badly. I don't have a driver's license or passport. But will this do?" I showed the porter the cover of the book. The porter shouted out, "The man knows Don Shula! Put him in first class." (Of course, Southwest doesn't have first class.) Everyone out by the curb began to give me high-fives. I was treated like a hero. Then one of the baggage handlers said, "Why don't I go into the terminal with you? I know the folks in security, and I think I can get you through there too."
>
> Why did that happen? Herb Kelleher, who founded Southwest Airlines, not only wanted to give the customers the lowest possible price, but he wanted to give them the best possible service. He set up the whole organization to empower everyone—right from the

frontline baggage check post—to make decisions, use their brains, and be customer service maniacs so they could create raving fans.

Kelleher (who has recently retired turned over the presidency of Southwest Airlines to his former executive secretary, Colleen Barrett) believes that policy should be followed but that people could use their brains in interpreting. Why do you ask for identification at the airport? To make sure that the person getting on the plane is the same person as the name on the ticket. That was an easy decision for the employee of Southwest.

The next airline I had to go to before my office could overnight my driver's license was an airline that is in financial trouble. The baggage handler at the curbside check-in looked at the book and said, "You've got to be kidding me. You'd better go to the ticket counter."

When I showed the book to the woman at the ticket counter, she said, "You'd better talk to my supervisor." I was moving up the hierarchy fast. I thought maybe soon I was going to get to the mayor and then finally the governor, Arnold Schwarzenegger. *Quack! Quack! Quack!*

In a troubled airline, the hierarchy was alive and well. All the energy was moving away from pleasing the customer and moving toward following the policy and procedures, rules, and regulations to the letter.

Jesus was often confronted with "quacking" behavior from the Pharisees and leaders of the synagogues. These religious leaders were more interested in protecting rules and regulations than hearing Jesus' message of love, forgiveness, and grace. For example:

On a Sabbath Jesus was teaching in one of the synagogues, and a woman was there who had been crippled by a spirit for eighteen years. She was bent over and could not straighten up at all. When Jesus saw her, he called her forward and said to her, "Woman, you are set free from your infirmity." Then he put his hands on her, and immediately she straightened up and praised God.

Indignant because Jesus had healed on the Sabbath, the synagogue ruler said to the people, "There are six days for work. So come and be healed on those days, not on the Sabbath."

The Lord answered him, "You hypocrites! Doesn't each of you on the Sabbath untie his ox or donkey from the stall and lead it out to give it water? Then should not this woman, a daughter of Abraham, whom Satan has kept bound for eighteen long years, be set free on the Sabbath day from what bound her?"

When he said this, all his opponents were humiliated, but the people were delighted with all the wonderful things he was doing. (Luke 13:10–17)

As a Lead Like Jesus leader, you don't want to nurture ducks. You want the leadership pyramid turned upside down so that those closest to the people you serve can soar like eagles.

Servant leadership really applies to your behavior during implementation, because now your job is to be *responsive* to your people and to help them to be responsible for living according to the vision, accomplishing the goals, and taking care of the customers.

Application Beyond Formal Organizations

While we have been focusing on the two roles of servant leadership in a formal organizational context, we want to be clear that these same two aspects of leadership play out in your life role leadership position in your family, church, and volunteer organization. For example, in a family, the parents are responsible to set the vision and goals for the family. As the kids get older, they can become involved in this process, but it is the parents' responsibility to provide the visionary role of leadership.

Unfortunately, many parents do not focus much attention on defining a positive vision for their family that everyone can understand. As a result, kids learn more about what *not* to do than how to do the right thing in the right way. A great source of frustration in families is what we call the "bring me a rock" syndrome. It occurs when a parent issues a nonspecific instruction like "Bring me a rock" but fails to test for understanding and becomes annoyed with results that don't meet their expectations. Implementation can only be effective if the important visionary work and goal setting is done first. Then the parents can move to the bottom of the hierarchy and serve the family vision.

For those who follow Jesus of Nazareth, the command for each and every person has already been established and communicated from the Father to all His children: "Love the Lord your God with all your heart and with all your soul and with all your mind and with all your strength" and "Love your neighbor as yourself" (Mark 12:30–31).

In the realm of one-on-one relationships, if you're seeking to lead like Jesus, your vision should always be committed service to the best interests of the other person. The way of committed service is not catering to the whims and individual preferences of the moment but seeking to respond to and encourage the best in someone else, not exploiting knowledge of their weakness and shortcomings for your own purposes. The term *tough love* speaks to a special kind of committed service that requires denial of support of destructive tendencies in the service of growth and development.

Clarify Your Personal Purpose

Before trying to influence and engage others in working with you to create a compelling vision, you need to be clear about your personal purpose. The leader's personal purpose must guide and align the efforts of those who are to follow, or their whole relationship is built on a false foundation. Hidden motives and hidden agendas will sabotage trust—the key ingredient in any leader-follower relationship.

What do we mean by your purpose in life? It means your reason for being, something you seek to fulfill as you move through your life. A purpose is different from a goal in that it does not have a beginning or an end; it is the meaning of the journey, not the destination. Purpose is bigger than any achievement. Your personal purpose is your calling—the reason you were created. In the context of leadership, being sure of your individual purpose in relationship to your influence on other people must include serving their best interests or it becomes manipulation and exploitation, the absolute opposite of leading like Jesus.

Jesus' Personal Purpose—Servant Leadership

A key insight into Jesus' leadership point of view is contained in His prayer for His disciples, recorded in John 17. It is worthwhile for us to

The fruit of great servant leadership is realized when a leader seeks to send the next generation of leaders to meet the challenges of their season with all the wisdom, knowledge, and spiritual resources he or she can provide.

reflect on the following points contained in this wonderful prayer of accountability of the ultimate servant leader.

Jesus stayed personally focused on what He was sent to accomplish in His season of leadership. He told His Father, "I brought glory to you here on earth by doing everything you told me to do" (John 17:4 NLT). In total obedience and commitment, Jesus stayed on point. He did not seek to take on other tasks or the agenda others hoped He would fulfill.

One of the greatest services a leader can provide to his or her followers is constancy of purpose. When the going gets rough or temptations and distractions come with short-term success or setbacks, people will look to the leaders to see how they will respond. Will they stay on course and remain true to their mission and values, or will they give up and give in to the pressures of the moment?

Pause and Reflect

As a leader, list three things that are most likely to pull you off course. What impact does changing course or direction have on the morale of the people you lead?

Jesus took accountability for going beyond proclamation in equipping His followers with a full understanding of what they needed to know to carry out their mission. "Now they know that everything I have is a gift from you, for I have passed on to them the words you gave me; and they accepted them and know that I came from you, and they believe you sent me" (John 17:7–8). When leaders fail to take the time and effort to ensure that what they have in mind is understood and accepted, they leave themselves open to frustration, an unfulfilled mission, and bewildered and discouraged followers. Investing the time to test for understanding and being willing to reinforce your intentions with repetition, repetition, repetition are signs of great leadership.

It is profoundly significant that the last lesson Jesus taught His disciples on the night of His betrayal was the same one He began with—what it means to be a servant leader. In Luke 22, we read,

> He took bread, gave thanks and broke it, and gave it to them, saying, "This is my body given for you; do this in remembrance of me." In the same way, after the supper he took the cup, saying, "This cup is the new covenant in my blood, which is poured out for you." . . . A dispute arose among them as to which of them was considered to be the greatest. Jesus said to them, "The kings of the Gentiles lord it over them; and those who exercise authority over them call themselves Benefactors. But you are not to be like that. Instead, the greatest among you should be like the youngest, and the one who rules like the one who serves." (vv. 19–20, 24–26)

Pause and Reflect

Think for a moment on the depth of character and the love Jesus displayed in that intense moment for His disciples, who within hours would abandon and deny Him. He did not give in to the temptation to despair over their slowness to grasp the essence of what He had repeatedly taught them about how they should lead. As the ultimate servant leader, Jesus demonstrated His willingness to provide what the disciples needed most to grow and develop in their ability to fulfill their mission, which was to be taught one more time.

Jesus displayed a high sense of accountability for the ongoing protection of His followers as He inspired and equipped them for their mission. He told His Father, "While I was with them, I protected them and kept them safe by that name you gave me. None has been lost except the one doomed to destruction, so that Scripture would be fulfilled" (John 17:12).

The more difficult and perilous the journey, the more willing a leader must be to maintain constant vigilance to the health and safety of his or her followers. This can take the form of making sure they are properly trained and equipped for their mission. It can mean providing and modeling a clear set of operating values to guide them in making decisions when the leader is not there. It can mean standing up for them in the face of opposition or unjustified criticism. It can also mean being a good guardian of their trust by telling them the truth and being willing to serve them in areas they are not yet able to accomplish on their own. As the Good Shepherd, Jesus laid down His life so that none might perish (John 10:11, 28).

Jesus looked beyond His season of leadership and sought to provide for His followers as they continued to implement the mission He commissioned them to fulfill. On the last night of His ministry on earth, Jesus prayed,

> Now I am departing the world; I am leaving them behind and coming to you. Holy Father, keep them and care for them —all those you have given to me—so that they will be united just as we are. . . . I'm not asking that you take them out of the world, but that you keep them safe from the evil one. (John 17:11, 15 NLT)

A truly great and enduring vision will extend beyond the leadership season of any one individual and be carried in the hearts and minds of those to whom it has been entrusted.

The fruit of great servant leadership is realized when a leader seeks to send the next generation of leaders to meet the challenges of their season with all the wisdom, knowledge, and spiritual resources he or she can provide. It is of the greatest significance and encouragement that the prayer Jesus offered on behalf of His first disciples, He offered as well for those who would come after them, including those who follow Him today. "My prayer is not for them alone. I pray also for those who will believe in me through their message" (John 17:20).

The "tyranny of the *or*" suggests that you, as a leader, have to choose results or people. Yet Jesus modeled a "both/and" point of view. In His daily interactions, He elevated the growth and development of people to the status of an end goal as important as achieving other results. Jesus did exactly what His Father called Him to do, and He also focused on the development of the people around Him.

In your own season of leadership, you are called to deal with the same reality. Following Jesus and leading as He led will mean you are serving a higher purpose and being held accountable at a higher level in a way that will not be universally understood or applauded. At the same time, you will do as He did and focus on serving people by helping them grow and develop.

The Vision of Servant Leadership

When Ken was a college professor, he was constantly in trouble with the school's faculty and was even investigated by faculty committees. The thing that drove the school officials crazy was that Ken always gave out the final exam questions on the first day of class. His reasoning was that he would not only give the exam questions to the students ahead of time, but he would spend the rest of the semester teaching them the answers because life is all about getting As, not some normal distribution curve.

Bob Buford, founder of Leadership Network and author of the book *Halftime*, believes that all of us are going to face a "final exam" when we stand before God at the end of our lives. According to Buford, the two questions on God's "final exam" will be:

1. What did you do with Jesus?
2. What did you do with the resources you were given in life?

When you know the questions ahead of time, there is no excuse not to get an A.

Most teachers have their students guess what will be on the final exam. Not so with Jesus. He was clear about the final exam and ready to help His followers get the right answer. He wanted everyone to get an A.

Jesus said, "The Son of Man did not come to be served, but to serve" (Matthew 20:28). What did He come to serve? He came to serve the vision He had been given by His Father. He came as a teacher, as a leader, and as a trainer to prepare people to go out and help other people live according to that vision. To do so, He served the people.

Chuck Colson, founder of Prison Fellowship, once pointed out during a speech, "All the kings and queens I have known in history sent their people out to die for them. I only know one King who decided to die for His people." That's the ultimate in servant leadership. Jesus isn't asking us literally to die for our people. But He's saying, "Not so with you" (Matthew 20:26) in terms of traditional leadership. He's mandating that we set a clear vision that is going to help the world.

The vision has to be something bigger than you are. Once that's set, the Lord's mandate is servant leader behavior. Servant leadership starts with a vision and ends with a servant heart that helps people live according to that vision.

Leading People Like Jesus Did

When we put the *heart* and the *head* together in a Lead Like Jesus perspective, people come to the forefront and self takes a backseat. Jesus knew His people intimately, He respected them profoundly, and He equipped them to be competent and confident leaders.

Now that you understand the two internal domains—*heart* and *head*—remember that servant leadership involves:

- Setting the purpose or vision
- Communicating a compelling picture of the future
- Defining and modeling the values, structure, and behavior you want from people
- Creating an environment of empowerment
- Moving to the bottom of the pyramid to support those who are responsible to serve
- Showing respect for everyone
- Placing the growth and development of people on par with accomplishing the vision

Jesus did all these things. He was clear about why He came, what the good news was, and what He wanted people to do. Then He modeled implementing servant leadership with everyone He met.

Pause and Reflect

Think for a moment about how well you serve those around you. Do you initiate coaching? Do you help your people to pass the final exam? Do you help them to live according to the vision? Leadership is not about power. It's not about control; it's about helping people live according to the vision.

It's the vision—the purpose, the picture of the future, and the values—that everyone should serve. To do that requires leaders to have a servant heart and a strategy to develop and empower others to live according the established vision, values, and goals.

That leads us to the first external domain—the *hands*, or our public leadership behavior. We will examine the *hands* of a servant leader in the next chapter.

Summary

- The journey of servant leadership that starts in the *heart* must then travel through the *head*, which is the leader's belief system and perspective on the role of the leader.
- There are two parts to the servant leadership that Jesus exemplified:
    1. A visionary role—setting the course and the destination

2. An implementation role—doing things right with a focus on serving

- A compelling vision tells people who they are, whose they are, where they are going, and what will guide their journey.
- Once your vision is set, you can then establish goals to answer the question, "What do you want people to focus on now?"
- When servant leadership begins, the traditional pyramid hierarchy must be turned upside down.
- Before trying to influence and engage others in working with you to create a compelling vision, you need to be clear about your own personal purpose.
- Servant leadership starts with a vision and ends with a servant heart that helps people live according to that vision.

Chapter 4

THE HANDS OF A SERVANT LEADER

Leading like Jesus is more than a theory; it's about changing the way you lead others. It means making a commitment to change your behavior to be more like Jesus. It means starting to ask yourself, "What would Jesus do?" before you act as a leader.

Laurie Beth Jones once shared a story about a leadership principle her friend learned while helping her two grandchildren carve pumpkins. Laurie's friend laid out several types of knives, and her grandson happily carved away, creating elaborate designs and even feet for his pumpkin. But her granddaughter wasn't quite old enough to handle certain knives, so the friend told her, "Honey, here's the one knife you can use to carve your pumpkin." The young girl protested, "But Grandma, I don't want to carve a pumpkin that doesn't go anywhere! I want it to have feet!"

Likewise, we don't want those of you reading this book to be "happy-face" Christians who simply recite a theory of leadership to others. Our desire is that you will learn how to put "feet" to your message by changing your behavior to be more like Jesus.

Do Self-Serving Leaders Ever Become Servant Leaders?

You may be wondering, "Do self-serving leaders ever just see the light and suddenly become servant leaders and stay that way?" First of all, you have to remember that we are all self-serving to some extent in some situations and relationships. Even someone whom everyone applauds as a servant leader will have moments when his or her ego gets in the way. If a person is a true-blue self-serving leader, it may be hard to turn them around but not hopeless.

We have found three ways that self-serving leaders can see the light and begin to make efforts to serve rather than to be served. The first way is by having a near-death experience. Interestingly, when people know they have been given a second chance and are on borrowed time, they seem to mellow. We call that the "Scrooge phenomenon." When people get in touch with their own mortality, they often see things differently and start to realize that life is more about what you give than what you get and serving rather than being served.

A second way people begin to see their lives and leadership differently is through a spiritual awakening. That is why we are so committed to inspiring and equipping people to lead like Jesus. That transformation cannot take place without developing a relationship with Jesus. When people start to walk with Him, He will call in a consistent voice for them to shed their self-serving habits and do as He would do.

That leads to the third factor that contributes to transformation: having a significant role model. If people are around a servant leadership role model often enough, the servant leader's behavior begins to rub off. That is why in our Lead Like Jesus ministry, we constantly turn to the Bible for examples that illustrate the unparalleled model of a servant heart that Jesus brought into this world. Above all, servant leaders care about people and want them to flourish and succeed in fulfilling their unique purpose and calling.

The Servant Leader as a Performance Coach

A key activity of an effective servant leader is to act as a performance coach. When Jesus called His disciples to follow Him, He pledged them His full support and guidance as they developed into "fishers of men." This is the duty of a servant leader—the ongoing investment of the leader's life into the lives of those who follow.

By being a performance coach and changing His leadership style appropriately as His disciples developed individually and as a group, Jesus empowered His followers to carry on after He was gone. Through His *hands* (effective leader behavior), Jesus was able to transmit to His disciples what was in His *heart* and *head* about servant leadership.

There are three parts to becoming a performance coach: performance planning, day-to-day coaching, and performance evaluation. Performance planning is all about providing direction and setting goals. Day-to-day coaching involves helping people win—accomplish their goals—by observing their performance, praising progress, and redirecting efforts that are off base. That leads to the third part of performance coaching: performance evaluation. That requires sitting down with people and evaluating their performance over time.

Which of these three activities do you think gets the most attention and effort by managers? Most people guess performance evaluation. Unfortunately, that is the truth.

Why? Because that is when leaders are expected to evaluate, judge, and sort out their people. If they rated all of their people high, these leaders would be rated low. They would be accused of being "too easy" or "giving away the farm." As a result, the normal distribution curve is alive and well. Managers are expected to rate only a few people high, a few people low, and the rest are considered average performers. Yet when we ask managers, "How many of you go out and hire losers so you can fill the low spots?" everyone laughs because they hire either winners—people who already have a good track record in what they want them to do—or potential winners—people who they think can become winners with proper coaching. They don't hire losers. Then why do a certain number of people have to lose—get rated low? Jesus certainly didn't believe in a normal distribution curve. He wanted everyone to win by realizing the truth of the good news He came to share.

In Ken's teaching example, performance planning is giving people the final exam ahead of time. In this aspect of performance coaching the traditional hierarchical pyramid can stay upright. Why? Because if there is a disagreement over goals, who wins? The leader does because he or she represents the organizational goals.

When Moses went to the top of the mountain to get the Ten Commandments, he didn't take a committee with him. Otherwise, he would have come down with three commandments and seven suggestions. Jesus didn't involve His disciples much in the goals He had come to accomplish. He got those from the top of the hierarchy—from His Father.

That does not mean that in our work in the home, community, and office, we shouldn't involve others in setting goals. You certainly can at work, with experienced people, and at home, when the kids get older. But it is each organizational or life role leader's responsibility to make sure direction is clear. In the life role leadership in a family, the parents have to take responsibility for setting goals and objectives. We all remember times when we would say to our mothers, "All of the other kids are doing it." If your mother was like ours, her response was always quick: "That's because their name isn't Blanchard (or Hodges)." Our parents were in charge of performance planning.

We can't emphasize enough the importance of clarity of purpose in the planning for the performance role of a servant leader. If there is not clear communication of what a good job will look like when it is accomplished, somebody will end up frustrated—either the leader or the follower or both.

Pause and Reflect

Think back to a time when you were on either side of a failure in communication on what was expected and what was delivered. Recall the frustration and wasted energy that could have been avoided by testing for understanding.

When it comes to day-to-day coaching, the hierarchy starts to turn upside down, and servant leaders begin to work for their people. At that point, the goals are clear, and a servant leader's main focus is helping people accomplish their goals—in other words, it is about teaching people the right answers. If that is not so, the traditional hierarchy is kept in place and all of the energy of the organization is moving away from the customers and up the hierarchy. Now pleasing the boss becomes the goal, because he or she is the key to a good performance review. In a family, after goals are set, the parents become cheerleaders, encouragers, and supporters of their kids in accomplishing their goals.

While a few organizations do a good job of performance planning, unfortunately in most instances, after goals are set, they often get filed away and forgotten until the end of the year, when managers are told to evaluate performance. Then there is the frantic running around trying to find the goals. That is an environment where it is difficult to be a servant leader. Why? Because day-to-day coaching is the least-used component of the three-part management system!

Coaching is the most important servant leadership element in helping people to accomplish their goals.

Once goals are clear, servant-hearted leaders should be available to teach people the answers, so when these people get to the final exam, most of them get As. After all, for servant leaders, whether they are organizational or life role leaders, life is all about helping people get As. They aren't threatened by people around them who perform well. They want their people to win.

The big question people ask is, "How do you help people get As?" In other words, how do you grow kids up to be responsible citizens? For the answer to that question, we can follow how Jesus transformed His disciples from untrained novices to master teacher apostles. In doing so, we will use the framework of development that Jesus had assuredly experienced as He was led through learning the carpenter trade from His earthly father, Joseph.

The Leadership Journey from Call to Commission

The Call
"Come, follow me, . . . and I will make you fishers of men . . ." (Matthew 4:19).

The Commission
"Go and make disciples of all nations, baptizing them in the name of the Father and of the Son and of the Holy Spirit, and teaching them to obey everything I have commanded you. And surely I am with you always, to the very end of the age" (Matthew 28:19–20).

When Jesus first called the disciples from their ordinary occupations to become "fishers of men," each brought life experiences and skills to this new task but no practical knowledge of how to fulfill this new role. After spending three years under the leadership of Jesus, the disciples were transformed from untrained novices to fully equipped, inspired, and spiritually grounded leaders able to fulfill the Great Commission to go to all nations with the good news.

How did Jesus accomplish the transition from call to commission? Although miracles were involved, the process was not miraculous. It entailed a perfect execution of a familiar process by a leader personally committed to accomplishing a goal through the growth and development of those who follow. We believe the experience Jesus had as a learner, under instruction as a carpenter, provided Him with a practical model for growing and developing people that He was able to use to guide the learning experience of His disciples from call to commission.

Having presumably been guided through four normal stages of learning a new task—from *novice* (someone just starting out) to *apprentice* (someone in training) to *journeyman* (someone capable of working independently) and finally *master/teacher* (someone highly skilled and able to teach others) of the carpenter craft—Jesus brought to His season of leadership a clear understanding of the journey from dependence to independence.

To progress from being a novice to becoming a master in any role or skill, learners need someone to guide them along the way and to give them what they need to advance through the learning process.

Novices enter the learning process through an orientation phase and then progress to a training phase as *apprentices* until they gain sufficient command of the work to proceed on their own. *Journeymen*, over time, develop the experience and advanced knowledge required to be endorsed and commissioned as *master/teachers*.

Novice	Apprentice	Journeyman	Master
Learning Stage			

The Needs of a Novice

Novices are people who are just starting out to perform a particular task or to accomplish an assigned goal. They need to know what, when, where, why, and how to do something.

A novice needs the leader to provide basic information. Phil remembers the first day of coming to a new school as a freshman in a new town. Walking in the door, he had little need for the information contained in an advanced geometry book; he needed someone to show him where his locker was and how to get to the restroom and cafeteria. Thirty years later, on the day he started to work in a high-rise office building as the new head of the personnel department, the most important things he needed to know were the location of his office and how to get to the restroom and the cafeteria.

Novices need basic information before they can progress. Novices also need someone committed to their development to welcome them into the learning process. They need to feel that someone "in the know" thinks their work is important enough to invest time and energy to teach it right.

The quickest way to turn off a novice is to delegate their orientation to someone who could care less about the success of the student. Have you ever gone through a registration process for something and been left in the clutches of a sleepy-eyed, monotone admission clerk on the verge of succumbing to a case of terminal boredom? Then you know what it feels like to be a novice and to be left in the supervision of an uncaring person.

When people begin a new task or goal as novices, they can be either excited about the opportunity or hesitant because they have been compelled into the learning process. For example, let's look at two parallel experiences: a fifteen-year-old girl learning to drive a car and a fifty-eight-year-old man learning to use a three-legged cane after suffering a stroke.

The day the teenager gets her learner's permit to drive, she is filled with excitement but has little knowledge about driving a car. So her father needs to tell her the exact sequence of things to do before turning on the ignition on her first test-drive. The day the stroke victim first encounters the rehab nurse to learn to walk with a cane, he is filled with anger and embarrassment on having to learn to do something he has been doing all his life but in a new and unattractive way.

Both novices have to follow instructions that may be new or awkward. In the case of the teenager, a glamorized view of herself driving her friends to the beach after one or two lessons may cause her to be overconfident and prone to impatience with the learning process. In the case of the stroke victim, the "why" question may cause him to be reluctant to come to terms with the new reality in his life.

Pause and Reflect

Think of a time when you were an untrained novice just starting out to learn a new task or role. What did you need most from someone else to help you get started? Did you get it? If not, what was the result?

Jesus and the Novice Disciples

The disciples were certainly novices when Jesus first encountered them.

> As Jesus was walking beside the Sea of Galilee, he saw two brothers, Simon called Peter and his brother Andrew. They were casting a net into the lake, for they were fishermen. "Come, follow me," Jesus said, "and I will make you fishers of men." At once they left their nets and followed Him. (Matthew 4:18–20)

Jesus saw in these hardworking fishermen the raw material for the future leaders of His ministry, which He would leave in their care when His earthly season of leadership was completed. In their enthusiasm,

Peter and Andrew literally dropped what they were doing when Jesus called them to the higher purpose of being "fishers of men."

Although they were enthusiastic, they had no idea of how to accomplish their new task. Remember, the task was to be "fishers of men"—not fishermen. Their learning stage was that of novices. At that stage of learning, they were dependent on Jesus to teach them about the new task. Therefore, to meet their learning needs, Jesus focused on telling them what to do and how to do it.

That's what Jesus did when He sent the twelve disciples out for the first time to preach the good news. He gave them extensive basic instructions on where to go, what to say, what to do, and how to do it:

> Do not go among the Gentiles or enter any town of the Samaritans. Go rather to the lost sheep of Israel. As you go, preach this message: The kingdom of heaven is near." Heal the sick, raise the dead, cleanse those who have leprosy, drive out demons. Freely you have received, freely give. Do not take along any gold or silver or copper in your belts; take no bag for the journey, or extra tunic, or sandals or a staff: for a worker is worth his keep.
>
> Whatever town or village you enter, search for some worthy person there and stay at his house until you leave. As you enter the home, give it your greeting. If the home is deserving, let your peace rest on it; if it is not, let your peace return to you. . . . I am sending you out like sheep among wolves. Therefore be as shrewd as snakes and as innocent as doves. (Matthew 10:5–13, 16)

We believe that leaders in churches and in business often set people up for failure because they do not accept responsibility for recognizing and responding effectively to this orientation learning stage.

The Needs of an Apprentice

Apprentices are people in training who have not yet mastered all the information and skills to work alone. They need to be assured that they are doing the right thing in the right way and to be corrected when they don't quite "have it." They also need someone to put their progress in the right perspective so they don't become overconfident with early success or discouraged with initial failure.

For example, the teenager learning to drive who has effectively fastened her seat belt and started the car on one of her practice runs begins to cry when she starts to pull out into traffic and is startled by a car racing by that she did not see. Her father needs to praise her for fastening her seat belt and turning on the car correctly, but he also needs her to repeat back to him how the mirrors are to be adjusted and how she must look both ways to anticipate the flow of traffic.

The stroke victim learning to walk with a three-legged cane starts off well enough for a few steps, but then he becomes frustrated and angry at the fact that it takes him many minutes to travel a distance he could previously cover in seconds. The rehab nurse needs to praise him for what he has accomplished so far but still direct his efforts and put his rate of progress in perspective.

Pause and Reflect

Think of a time when you needed someone to push you beyond a failure or an easy early success to get to a higher level of understanding and performance in a new task. Think of a time when you quit because nobody was there to take you to the next level.

Jesus and the Apprentice Disciples

Jesus had to respond to a number of situations with His disciples as they were apprenticing with Him. For example, the disciples were discouraged when they were unable to cast a demon out of a boy whom a father brought to them. Casting out demons was one of the tasks Jesus had assigned to the disciples in Matthew 10, when He sent them out. In Matthew 17:15–16, we read of a man who pleads with Jesus to heal his son. "Lord, have mercy on my son," he said. "He has seizures and is suffering greatly. He often falls into the fire or into the water. I brought him to your disciples, but they could not heal him."

When the disciples were new to the task of being "fishers of men," they experienced a setback to their confidence when they discovered they were not competent to handle every situation. Think how the disciples must have felt when they were not able to succeed at casting out the demon from the boy. They must have been frustrated, uncertain, and embarrassed.

Your people or family members or volunteers may experience those same feelings when confronted with a task or a goal they cannot do or in which they experienced a failure or problem. Sometimes the people you lead become discouraged about a specific task while you as a leader are completely unaware of their disillusionment. If people become disillusioned and no one reaches out to them, they can become so discouraged that they quit and leave. Sometimes they will stay on the job but express their disillusionment by just going through the motions, which negatively affects the enthusiasm and commitment of others. In other words, they may quit and stay. Kids will stay living at home but mentally drop out and not share any personal information or concerns with their parents.

Observe how Jesus responded to His disciples' disillusionment over not being able to cast out the demon. In Matthew 17:18–20, we read,

> Jesus rebuked the demon, and it came out of the boy, and he was healed from that moment. Then the disciples came to Jesus in private and asked, "Why couldn't we drive it out?" He replied, "Because you have so little faith. I tell you the truth, if you have faith as small as a mustard seed, you can say to this mountain, 'Move from here to there' and it will move. Nothing will be impossible for you."

Notice that Jesus gave the disciples truthful information as to why they were unable to cast out the demon: "Because you have so little faith."

Jesus tells the disciples that the casting out of these demons comes only out of prayer and fasting.[1] We know that Jesus loved His disciples and wanted them to succeed (John 17:6–19). We also know Jesus was "without sin" (Hebrews 4:15), which means He never lost control of His temper in a sinful manner. Even when the disciples had failed and He came behind them to "clean up their mess," He still loved them and expressed that love by telling them the truth in a loving way.

Now what does this say to you as a leader trying to lead like Jesus during the training phase with apprentices? It is vital that you provide clear direction and information in a loving manner. If you are to follow the example of Jesus as a leader, never demean people or try to make them feel inferior because of a failure on their part. As Jesus did, you should let the love you have for those with whom you work come through and let your desire to lead like Jesus always direct your behavior.

The Needs of a Journeyman

It is easy to assume that journeymen—people who have acquired well-developed skills in performing a task or role—have progressed to a point where all they need from a leader is to be told when and where to apply their skills. The fact of the matter is that they may periodically become cautious, lose confidence, or have a diminished sense of enthusiasm for the job due to a variety of reasons. If ignored by inattentive leaders, journeymen quietly drift into apathy or retreat from taking risks due to a feeling of lost competence or connection with their calling.

Journeymen can lose their skills and ability to perform and become disillusioned critics and skeptics who poison the attitude of those who work around them. Leaders who ignore the needs of journeymen for appreciation, encouragement, and inspiration do so at their peril.

An example of a leader meeting the needs of a journeyman is a father who hugs his teenage daughter after she becomes nervous and fails her first driving test even though she received an A in drivers' education. Once she regains her composure, he encourages her to take the wheel and drive them home. Another example is a rehab nurse who reminds the stroke victim of how far he has come in gaining his new skill and how proud of him she is as he prepares to use his cane in front of his family and friends.

Pause and Reflect

Has there ever been a time when you felt underappreciated or unrecognized for a job well done because the attention was being given to the "problem children"? What would have been the effect of a leader reinforcing you with some small heartfelt sign of appreciation?

Jesus and a Journeyman Disciple

Peter exhibited behaviors characteristic of a journeyman when he walked on water. In Matthew 14:26–30, we read,

> When the disciples saw him [Jesus] walking on the lake, they were terrified. "It's a ghost," they said, and cried out in fear. But Jesus immediately said to them, "Take courage! It is I. Don't be afraid." "Lord, if it's you," Peter replied, "tell me to come to you on the water." "Come," he said. Then Peter got down out of the boat, walked on the water and came toward Jesus. But when he saw the wind, he was afraid and, beginning to sink, cried out, "Lord, save me!"

Peter is a great illustration of someone capable of performing the task at hand as he steps on the water and begins to walk. It took a tremendous amount of faith for Peter to step out of the boat and onto the water. So often we focus on Peter's cry for help that we forget that Peter actually did walk on water! In fact, he is the only one besides Jesus who has ever done such a thing. Peter's problem, though, came when he took his eyes off Jesus and began to worry about the storm. When Peter's confidence moved from high to low, his demonstrated competence sank into the water with him.

Jesus was there to provide the support Peter needed when he started to sink, even though he had demonstrated the ability to walk on water. "Immediately Jesus reached out his hand and caught him. 'You of little faith,' he said, 'why did you doubt?' And when they climbed into the boat, the wind died down" (vv. 31–32).

What can we learn from the response of Jesus as a leader when Peter sank into the water? First, we notice that Jesus acted immediately. He did not let Peter sink into the water and think about his mistake. Jesus let Peter know immediately that He was there to give the support Peter needed.

Next, we observe that Jesus "reached out His hand and caught him" (v. 31). He used a personal touch to save the drowning apostle. Jesus knew that Peter's primary need was support, so He used His hand to save him. He reinforced His continued support of Peter when He said, "You of little faith . . . why did you doubt?" (v. 31). In other words, Jesus reminded Peter—and us—that He is always there when we need Him.

It is also important to remember that after Jesus caught Peter, they were still outside the boat. The image we have of that scene is one where Jesus wraps His arms around Peter and walks him back into the boat. Providing support to the people around us is so key to their continual development whether in the office, the home or the community. Truett Cathy, founder of Chick-fil-A, is often heard to say, "Who needs encouragement?" His reply: "Anyone who is breathing!"

The Needs of a Master/Teacher

Master/teachers are people with fully developed skills, confidence, and motivation to produce excellent results as individual performers, as well as the wisdom and insight to teach others. They need to be given the opportunity and challenge to pass on what they know to the next generation of learners—and they need your blessing.

Examples of master/teachers include parents who allow their teenage daughter to drive their car to a downtown college interview and the rehab department calling on the stroke victim to demonstrate his skills with his cane and encourage new patients who need to make the same journey from dependence to independence that he did.

Pause and Reflect

Commissioning "to go and teach others in my name" is the highest form of recognition that a teacher can give a follower. Fulfilling the commission is the highest compliment and act of gratitude the student can afford the teacher. What are you doing to pass along that which has been given to you for the next generation?

Jesus and the Master/Teacher Disciples

Jesus desired for His disciples to be able to be fully inspired and fully equipped for the task of being "fishers of men." This is evident when we read about Peter spreading the good news in Acts 2:36–41:

> "God has made this Jesus, whom you crucified, both Lord and Christ." When the people heard this they were cut to the heart and said to Peter and the other apostles, "Brothers, what shall we do?" Peter replied, "Repent and be baptized, every one of you, in the name of Jesus Christ for the forgiveness of your sins. And you will receive the gift of the Holy Spirit. The promise is for you and your children and for all who are far off—for all whom the Lord our God will call." With many other words he warned them; and he pleaded with them, "Save yourselves from this corrupt generation." Those who accepted his message were baptized, and about three thousand were added to their number that day.

We can look at Peter again and see that, under the anointing of the Holy Spirit, he is a master/teacher as he speaks to a crowd of thousands, and three thousand are baptized that day. Peter has the knowledge to share the message of Jesus, and he also exhibits a high level of commitment as a master/teacher. Notice how Peter boldly shares the message of Jesus. He speaks with authority. He is a real "fisher of men."

What is your desire for the people who look to you for leadership: frustrated individuals who do not have the competence or commitment to accomplish the assigned task, or people who are not only able to do the task on their own but who can also teach others? Imagine the benefits of having people around you who are not only good at doing their jobs but also are willing and able to teach others.

Sending out someone to act on your behalf is the highest form of validation of your trust in that person's competence and commitment. For example, when Jesus gave the Great Commission to His disciples, He assumed they were master/teachers and ready to perform on their own as "fishers of men." He commissioned them to "go and make disciples of all nations, baptizing them in the name of the Father, and of the Son and of the Holy Spirit, and teaching them to obey everything I have commanded you" (Matthew 28:19–20). While Jesus would not be physically present to direct and support the disciples as He had for three years, He did not turn His back on them. He promised, "I am with you always, to the very end of the age" (v. 20). Jesus promised not to leave the disciples alone to accomplish their task of being "fishers of men." He promised He would always be available to them.

It is important not to confuse delegating with abdicating. Leaders who *abdicate* turn their backs on their people and do not gather information on their own. They only become involved again if they hear bad news. But leaders who *delegate* stay in the information loop and are ready to help if they are called. Jesus delegated, but He did not abdicate. Jesus knew His disciples would need Him in the future, and He was ready when they called to still support them when necessary.

Leader-Follower Partnership

For someone to advance from a novice to a master/teacher, that person needs a leadership partner who can give him or her whatever direction and support the learner needs to advance to the next learning stage. Thus, a successful learner-development process is a mutual commitment. The diagram below depicts that partnership relationship:

Leader/Teacher/Parent Provides			
Basic information: What, How, Where, When, Why	Instruction Practice, and Evaluation	Assignment and Encouragement	Affirmation and Autonomy
Novice (someone just starting out)	**Apprentice** (someone in training)	**Journeyman** (someone able to work independently)	**Master** (someone able to teach others)
Learning Stages			

It is important to know that the learning-stages process is not a global concept. No one is totally a novice, apprentice, journeyman, or master/teacher in the things he or she does. At any one time in our work life or in one of our life role relationships, we could be at all four learning stages. At work, you could be a novice on the new computer program, an apprentice on budgeting, a journeyman on people development, and a master at planning. As a result, a leadership partner not only must learn to use different strokes for different folks but will probably end up using different strokes with the same folks on different parts of their organizational or life role development. In school, a youngster may be great at reading but struggling at math. Using the same teaching style for both of these subjects with this child would be a disaster.

To create an effective leader-follower partnership certain things have to take place. Both leader and follower must

- Understand the learner stages and the follower needs at each stage
- Agree on goals and objectives for the follower
- Diagnose together the learning stage of the follower for each goal
- Determine together what the follower needs at each stage for each goal and how the leader will provide it
- Be aware of when the follower is shifting to a new learning stage and what that means to their relationship

Over forty years ago, Ken began developing Situational Leadership with Paul Hersey.[2] Today, the latest version of that concept, called Situational Leadership® II, is used widely around the world to help leaders develop high performing leader-follower relationships. It was not until the late 1980s when Ken became a believer and read the Bible that he realized how compatible the concepts contained in Situational Leadership® II were with the biblical record of how Jesus trained and developed His disciples as he moved them from Call to Commission.

The EGO Factor in Leader-Follower Relationships

A servant-hearted leader—whether in the office, at home, or in the community—who is confronted with a self-focused learner or follower faces the daily challenge to minister to the heart of the follower as well as to move the learning process along. When your leadership is challenged or your motives and methods are mistrusted, keeping your EGO in check can be a daunting chore. Reacting out of pride or fear can easily shortcut the learning process if you resort to exerting negative, position-driven power to exert your will.

On the other hand, a servant-hearted follower confronted with a self-focused leader faces the daily challenge to be a positive witness to the leader while continuing to acquire the skills and experience needed to be productive and grow. It can be done, but it may be a hard, uphill climb. An EGO-driven leader can create disillusionment and cynicism in even the most servant-hearted follower, resulting in an ineffective learning process.

The true test of servant leadership begins when the EGO of the leader and the EGO of the follower engage one another. How well they recognize and overcome the pride and fear factors in their relationship determines whether they move toward mutual satisfaction of commonly held goals or share in frustrations of their own making. *The following diagram is an effective tool in understanding leader (L)-follower (F) relationships:*

The EGO Factor in Leader-Follower Relationships

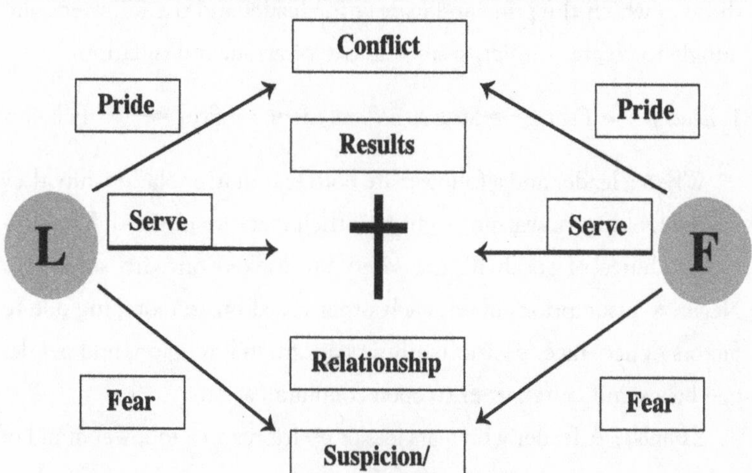

1. *Leader ⟶ Serve ⟶ Results and Relationship ⟵ Serve ⟵ Follower*

The ideal, most productive relationship between leader and follower occurs when a servant-hearted leader and a servant-hearted follower engage one another in an atmosphere of mutual service and trust. It is when a clear sense of purpose, process, and practice passes from the leader and is received and owned by the follower. The follower in turn responds with trust and willingness to perform and take instruction.

Example: Jesus glorified God by completing the work that had been set before Him to do (John 17:4).

Example: A parent and child who love and respect each other and both grow from their relationship.

Four Ineffective Leader-Follower Relationships

The four least effective relationships between leader and follower are those in which the pride and fears of the leader and the follower commingle to create conflict, suspicion, exploitation, and isolation.

1. *Leader* ⟶ *Fear* ⟶ *Suspicion/Paralysis* ⟵ *Fear* ⟵ *Follower*

When a leader and a follower are both fearful in a relationship, they will be looking for warning signs that their fears are justified. Even initial evidence of goodwill and safety are looked on with suspicion. Negative assumptions about each other based on stereotyping due to factors of age, race, position, ethnic background, religion, and gender can be a significant barrier to open communication.

Example: A leader who fears loss of position and a follower afraid of failure engage in a relationship of mutual suspicion. An older white male manager is assigned to train an image-conscious minority employee on a fast-track development program.

Example: A parent who wants his child to know he is in charge and a child who does not want to admit he has done something wrong.

2. *Leader* ⟶ *Pride* ⟶ *Conflict/Competition* ⟵ *Pride* ⟵ *Follower*

When a leader and a follower both bring their pride into a relationship, it is likely to become a test of wills. Instead of proceeding through cooperation and concessions, both parties seek to promote their position by winning arguments and tests of strength.

Example: A championship-winning coach with a ball-control strategy for winning meets a young superstar known for his brilliant individual skills.

Example: A parent who thinks she knows better what her teenage daughter could be doing and a teenager who is going through a know-it-all stage.

3. *Leader* ⟶ *Pride* ⟶ *Exploitation* ⟵ *Fear* ⟵ *Follower*

When a leader interested in imposing his will and his way on the people under his control as an extension of his self-importance plays on the insecurities of the follower, the results are not likely to be for the common good.

Example: A results-driven pastor intimidates his congregation into voting for a new sanctuary.

Example: A parent who wants his son to listen to him because he is a parent and a teenager who is fearful of being seen by his peers as a "mama's boy."

4. *Leader* ⟶ *Fear* ⟶ *Manipulation* ⟵ *Pride* ⟵ *Follower*

When an insecure leader succumbs to making unwise concessions or tries to exert position power to gain the cooperation of a strong-willed follower, the results are damaging.

Example: A micromanaging team leader who fears loss of control meets a prideful journeyman who responds with "malicious obedience" by complying with instructions that he knows are faulty.

Example: A parent who is afraid of the bad influences that may exist at school and a young son who is determined to demonstrate his independence.

Four Leader-Follower Relationships That Can Be Improved

There are four combinations of leader and follower EGOs that have specific challenges but can be improved if someone is willing to serve as an agent of change in the relationship. When that person is a leader, it is a ministry opportunity. When the change agent is the follower, it is a witnessing opportunity.

1. *Leader* → *Serve* → *Ministry* ← *Fear* ← *Follower*

A servant-hearted leader remains patient and reassuring by praising progress and honest effort when faced with followers who act out their insecurities.

Example: A physical therapist responds with patience and encouragement to outbursts of frustration and fear by a stroke victim learning to walk with a cane.

Example: A parent who is patient with a child who is having a temper tantrum.

2. *Leader* → *Serve* → *Ministry* ← *Pride* ← *Follower*

A servant-hearted leader models humility and strength of purpose and is willing to enforce standards and withstand challenges to his or her leadership.

Example: Jesus responds to the pride of His disciples arguing about who was to be greatest among them by washing their feet.

Example: A parent who does not get in a win/lose confrontation with a son over the family curfew.

3. *Leader* → *Pride* → *Witness* ← *Serve* ← *Follower*

A follower is willing to risk a negative response from a leader in order to uphold a principle or correct an error.

Example: The prophet Nathan confronts King David regarding his misconduct with Bathsheba.

Example: A child who confronts his father about his drinking and driving.

4. *Leader* ⟶ *Fear* ⟶ *Witness* ⟵ *Serve* ⟵ *Follower*

A follower responds to the insecurities of a leader with humility and respect without foregoing principle.

Example: As an expression of his allegiance and respect, David, while being pursued by a fear-driven King Saul, forgoes the opportunity to kill him when he had the chance.

Example: A child who is patient with a parent who is fearful about her going away to school.

Overcoming the EGO Factor in Leader-Follower Relationships

As a leader, the quickest remedy to the EGO factor in leader-follower relationships comes from seeking to acknowledge and combat your own vulnerabilities to pride and fear. The spiritual health of the leader is the wellspring from which a follower's trust and commitment flows. If you seek to inspire and equip others to higher standards of performance and commitment, the best first step is modeling integrity in your own journey toward the same direction.

As a follower whose self-worth and security is grounded in God's unconditional love and promises, keeping a big-picture perspective of what is to be gained or lost in responding to poor treatment by an EGO-driven leader can truly "turn lemons into lemonade."

A part of Ken's own spiritual journey provides an excellent example of the power of being a servant-hearted follower. After receiving his doctorate, Ken was working at Ohio University in Athens, Ohio, when he became aware of a course in organizational behavior and leadership taught by Paul Hersey, a brilliant and well-known professor whom Ken thought would benefit his own growth and development. When he inquired if it would be possible for him to audit the course, Hersey said, "No one audits my course! If you would like to take it for credit, you are welcome to do so."

Given the fact that Ken already had a PhD and Hersey did not, the temptation to let pride get in the way could have prevented Ken from learning some things that were to be vital to his career. With some wise encouragement from his wife, Margie, not to let his pride get in the way, Ken enrolled in Hersey's class as a regular student, taking the tests and writing the required papers. When the class was over, Hersey approached Ken with an invitation to collaborate with him in writing a textbook on organizational behavior because, "It's hard for me to sit still and write." Earlier in his career, Ken thought he would never be a writer because the faculty in his graduate program, in a kind way, said he would never be a writer.

In response to Hersey's invitation, Ken said, "We should make a great team—you can't sit still to write, and I'm not supposed to be able to write. So let's give it a try." The result of this collaboration was a classic textbook entitled *Management of Organizational Behavior*, which is now in its eighth edition. That book launched writing careers for Ken and Paul that have produced books that have sold millions of copies.

If both the leader and the follower are willing to share their own vulnerabilities and support one another in keeping on track, then the best of all results is possible—the true win-win-win situation: the leader wins, the follower wins, and God wins!

The EGO Factor in the Four Learning Stages

As we have emphasized, we all fall short of perfection, and every day we have to confront our own EGO issues that can get us off purpose and impact the leader and follower/learner relationship. So let's see if we can anticipate the EGO issues that leaders and followers face at each of the four learning stages:

EGO Issues at the Novice Stage

Learner/Novice EGO Issues	*Teacher/Leader EGO Issues*
Fear of failure	Impatience in teaching fundamentals
Fear of inadequacy	Frustration with slow progress
Fear of looking foolish	Temptation for premature delegation
False pride in position	Making quick judgments of potential
False pride due to prior performance	Fear of failure
Lack of trust in the leader or the method of training	

EGO Issues at the Apprentice Stage

Learner/Apprentice EGO Issues	*Teacher/Leader EGO Issues*
Discouragement with lack of progress	Fear of failure
Impatience with the learning process	Frustration with lack of enthusiasm
Loss of faith in the learning process	Unrealistic expectations of people
Fear of failure	Fear of the opinion of others
Fear of inadequacy	Fear of criticism

EGO Issues at the Apprentice Stage (cont'd)

Loss of faith in the leader	Fear of loss of position
Diminished enthusiasm for the task	

EGO Issues at the Journeyman Stage

Learner/Journeyman EGO Issues	*Teacher/Leader EGO Issues*
Fear of failure when moving into new situations	Lack of sensitivity to lost enthusiasm
Fear of success in expanded use of skills	Overuse of competence
Burnout—loss of enthusiasm and vision	Fear of intimacy required to deal with the individual issues
Fear of obsolescence	Fear of the learner surpassing the teacher
Fear of competition	
Fear of confronting slips in performance	
Fear of exploitation	

EGO Issues at the Master/Teacher Stage

Learner/Master EGO Issues	*Teacher/Leader EGO Issues*
Complacency with current knowledge of skills	Fear of personal competition from the fully inspired and equipped follower
Unwillingness to take criticism or direction	Fear of personal obsolescence when the learner can do what you do
Arrogance	Unwillingness to share information or recognition
Misuse of skills for self-serving purposes	Fear of loss of control

Aware of the potential EGO barriers in their relationship and willing to confront them, the leader and the follower can seek individually and together to overcome these barriers through personal preparation, open communication, and a mutual commitment to serve one another and their relationship. One unique resource at the disposal of the followers of Jesus is the active participation of the Holy Spirit as Counselor and Guide. Jesus promised in John 14:26, "The Counselor, the Holy Spirit, whom the Father will send in My name, will teach you all things and will remind you of everything I have said to you."

In chapter 7 there are a series of prayers for both leaders and followers as they progress from novice to master/teacher. We want to encourage you to use these preemptive prayers whenever you are about to enter a leader/learner situation. It will make a powerful difference.

Staying on Purpose

As we have emphasized, even if you, as a leader or follower/learner, are committed to serve rather than be served, every day your EGO is waiting to get you off course and focus your energy on being self-serving. In the following chapter, we will take a look at some of the habits that were essential to how Jesus renewed and reaffirmed His daily walk of submission and obedience as a servant and leader.

Summary

- A key activity of an effective servant leader is to act as a performance coach—making an ongoing investment into the lives of those who follow.

- There are three parts to becoming a performance coach: performance planning, day-to-day coaching, and performance evaluation. After goals and direction are clear, the focus of a servant leader is on day-to-day coaching—helping people get As.

- There are four stages of learning a new task or skill:
    1. Novice—someone just starting out
    2. Apprentice—someone in training
    3. Journeyman—someone capable of working on his own
    4. Master/teacher—someone highly skilled and able to teach others

- The role of the leader is the same throughout the transformation process—to provide what the learner needs to advance to the next stage.

- The true test of servant leadership begins when the EGO of the leader and the EGO of the follower engage one another.

Chapter 5

THE HABITS OF A SERVANT LEADER

We all have two selves. We have an external, task-oriented self that is used to getting jobs done, and we have an internal, more reflective self that is very thoughtful. Which of those two selves wakes up quicker in the morning: our external, task-oriented self or our internal, reflective self? Of course, it's our external, task-oriented self.

What happens in the morning? The alarm goes off! Have you ever thought about that phrase—*alarm clock*? What an awful concept. Why isn't it the "opportunity" clock? Or the "it's going to be a great day" clock? The "alarm" immediately ignites your task-oriented self, and you jump out of bed. Pretty soon you're trying to eat breakfast while you're washing. You race to the car and immediately pick up the cell phone and rush off to meetings all morning, followed by a lunch meeting, afternoon meetings, and a dinner meeting. Finally, you get home at 9:00 or 10:00 p.m. and fall into bed exhausted, without any energy to say goodnight to anybody who might be lying next to you. What happens the next day? The "alarm" goes off, and you're at it again. Pretty soon your life becomes a rat race. As Lily Tomlin once said, "The problem with a rat race is that even if you win, you're still a rat."

To avoid being consumed by the rat race and the pressure of life, all of us need to develop strategies and spiritual habits that will help us stay on purpose.

As Jesus moved through His season of earthly leadership, He was under constant pressure and temptation to get off course or respond to the failings of both His friends and His enemies. Jesus stayed on track with His mission by applying five key habits that countered the negative forces in His life:

1. Solitude
2. Prayer
3. Study and application of Scripture
4. Accepting and responding to God's unconditional love
5. Involvement in supportive relationships

Adopting these same habits is essential for those who seek to follow Jesus as their role model for leadership. He didn't try to lead without these five habits, and neither should we if we want to lead like Jesus. Without habits, life can stay a rat race.

And how do we become like Jesus? As Rick Warren says in *The*

If we want to lead like Jesus, we have to become like Jesus.

Purpose Driven Life, "Your character is essentially the sum of your habits."[1] If we want to develop a character like Jesus, we have to look carefully at His habits.

Jesus' habits included spending time in solitude and prayer, relying on the Word of God, having confidence in His unconditional love relationship with His Father, and benefiting from the comfort He found in fellowship with a small group of intimates. These habits flowed effortlessly from His very nature and permeated His daily walk and leadership. Yet most of us have to work at acquiring these disciplines before they become habits.

It would go beyond the scope of this book to provide a comprehensive study of all the vital aspects of the life we are called to as followers of Jesus. But it is important for us to encourage you to begin or renew your journey to developing these five disciplines as key ingredients to leading like Jesus. To do so, we will highlight what Jesus did. When you face a similar situation and may be prompted to ask, "What would Jesus do?" you will know where to look for the answer—in His habits.

The Habit of Solitude

Of the five habits we are going to discuss, solitude is by far the most elusive in our modern world of busyness and 24-7 communications. Solitude is a countercultural and challenging behavior. It draws us into the very place from which so much of our efforts are designed to help us escape—being truly alone with God without an agenda. It is a rare and often unsettling feeling to stop doing and just be. Yet as strange as it feels to actively seek opportunities to "cease striving" (Psalm 46:10 NASB), the result can be life changing.

Solitude is being completely alone with God away from all human contact for extended periods of time. It is like stepping out the back door of your noisy life of to-do lists and demanding relationships to breathe in some fresh air. Solitude is being refreshed and restored by the natural rhythms of life that are not impacted by your strivings or those of anyone else. It is taking time to listen for the "still small voice" in which God speaks to your soul and tells you that you are His beloved (1 Kings 19:12 KJV). Sometimes, doing nothing is the best thing you can do for your people and for yourself.

Jesus modeled solitude as an integral strategic component of His leadership. Consider the following:

- When preparing for the tests of leadership and public ministry, Jesus spent forty days alone in the desert. (Matthew 4:1–11)
- Before Jesus chose His twelve apostles from among His followers, He spent the entire night alone in the desert hills. (Luke 6:12–13)
- When Jesus received the news of the death of John the Baptist, He withdrew in a boat to a lonely place. (Matthew 14:13)
- After the miraculous feeding of the five thousand, Jesus went up in the hills by Himself. (Matthew 14:23)

It was in these times of preparing to lead, making important decisions, handling bad news, and dealing with praise and recognition that Jesus modeled for us the value of spending time alone to seek recalibration of our spiritual instruments for finding the "true north" of God's will and pleasure.

The most powerful example of the critical role that solitude played in the life and leadership of Jesus is described in John 6:14–15, where He was faced with a difficult choice in how best to use His time.

> After the people saw the miraculous sign that Jesus did, they began to say, "Surely this is the Prophet who is to come into the world."

> Jesus, knowing that they intended to come and make him king by force, withdrew again to a mountain by himself.

Success and the roar of the crowd can be intoxicating to a leader, especially to one who has bought into the idea that self-worth is equal to performance plus the opinion of others. Taking time alone with God as the audience of One is an important habit that will keep EGO from compromising your leadership. As Proverbs 27:21 says, "The crucible for silver and the furnace for gold, but man is tested by the praise he receives."

One of the most difficult challenges a leader faces is not to pay too much attention to either criticism or praise. We tend to agree with this advice concerning criticism, but we often ignore the advice about praise and recognition. As a leader, you face both.

Another important aspect of daily time with God in solitude is that it enables you to make the difficult choices of leadership. Jesus used the early morning hours to find solitude so that He could make the tough choices between the good use of His time and the best use of His time. In Mark 1:32–38, we read,

> That evening after sunset the people brought to Jesus all the sick and demon-possessed. The whole town gathered at the door, and Jesus healed many who had various diseases. He also drove out many demons, but he would not let the demons speak because they knew who he was.
>
> Very early in the morning, while it was still dark, Jesus got up, left the house and went off to a solitary place, where he prayed. Simon and his companions went to look for him, and when they found him, they exclaimed: "Everyone is looking for you!"

Jesus replied, "Let us go somewhere else—to the nearby villages—so I can preach there also. That is why I have come."

"Very early in the morning, while it was still dark, Jesus got up, left the house and went to a solitary place and prayed." These words stand between Jesus and the temptation to spend His precious time doing the good and popular thing instead of doing the primary work for which He had come. Imagine Jesus' intense compassion for the sick and demon-possessed people He would have to leave. Imagine how strong the temptation would have been for Him to stay and use His healing powers to the delight of all. His disciples expected Jesus to seize this opportunity because He was the Messiah who would call Israel to God. But they thought like men, and Jesus had just heard from His Father.

What allowed Jesus to resist doing this good work and pick the best? We believe that in solitude and prayer, away from the hopes and hurts of those who looked to Him with high and compelling expectations, that Jesus again received the answers of the best use of the next day from the Father.

In our Leadership Encounters, we ask participants to take forty-five minutes of solitude—a time when they do not talk to anyone, use their computer or BlackBerry, or allow any other distractions. We ask them to begin by putting their hands palms-down on their knees and thinking of anything they are concerned about. As a concern appears in their mind, they ceremonially put it down at the foot of the cross. When they have completed thinking about their concerns, they turn their hands upward in a posture of receiving and contemplate some aspect of the character of God, such as His mercy, His love, His grace, or His power. We instruct them to listen without any agenda. Before we send people off for their period of solitude, we have them recite with us Psalm 46:10 in this way:

Be still and know that I am God.

Be still and know.

Be still.

Be.

When people return from their time of solitude, they have big smiles on their faces. While many of them found it difficult to quiet their mind, they say it was a powerful experience.

The reality is most of us spend little if any time in solitude. Yet if we don't, how can God have a chance to talk with us?

Pause and Reflect

When was the last time you spent a significant amount of time in solitude on purpose without a to-do, think, or pray list and sat quietly in God's presence and listened to His "still, small voice?" If you can't remember, you now have a clue why your life and leadership seem so hindered and unsatisfying. If you can remember and it was more than a week ago, you need to update your plans for the immediate future.

The Habit of Prayer

If solitude is the most elusive of the habits for us to develop, prayer is the one that requires the most unlearning and revision of old habits and patterns.

The one thing that is most instructive about how and where leaders might take their followers is found in their prayer life. Prayer is an essential act of the will that demonstrates whether we are really serious about living and leading like Jesus. Without it, we will never be able to open the way for connecting our plans and efforts with God's plan for His kingdom or engaging the spiritual resources that Jesus promised in the work of the Holy Spirit. Seeking God's will through prayer, waiting in faith for an answer, acting in accordance with that answer, and being at peace with the outcome call for a level of spiritual maturity that will keep anyone seeking to lead like Jesus in the posture of a lifelong learner. The nature and objects of our prayers will determine whether we are being EGO-driven or are glorifying God.

In order to lead like Jesus, you will face some leadership challenges. Let's examine the example Jesus gave us to follow.

Jesus' Prayer in Gethsemane

Nowhere in the Bible is a model of praying like Jesus more powerfully provided for us than in the dark hours of the night before He was betrayed. This was a time when the temptation to abandon His mission was at an almost unbearable level:

> Jesus went with his disciples to a place called Gethsemane, and he said to them, "Sit here while I go over there and pray." He took Peter and the two sons of Zebedee along with him and he began to be sorrowful and troubled. Then he said to them, "My soul is overwhelmed with sorrow to the point of death. Stay here and keep watch with me."
>
> Going a little farther, he fell with his face to the ground and prayed, "My Father, if it is possible, may this cup be taken from me. Yet not as I will, but as you will." (Matthew 26:36–39)

Jesus' prayer in the garden of Gethsemane is an excellent example for leaders. Let's look at four instructive aspects of His prayer.

1. *Where did Jesus pray and why?* He went off by himself for prayer. A troubled soul finds the most ease when it is alone with God, who understands the broken language of sighs and groans. While alone with God, Jesus could freely pour out His heart to the Father without restraint.

2. *What was Jesus' posture in prayer?* He fell on His face before His Father, indicating His agony, extreme sorrow, and humility in prayer. At other times Jesus prayed looking up to heaven, with His eyes open, or kneeling. The posture of the heart is more important than the posture of the body, but prostrating our physical selves before God helps our heart posture.

3. *What did Jesus ask in prayer?* Jesus asked, "If it is possible, may this cup be taken from me" (v. 39). He was asking if He could avoid the suffering of the Cross. But notice the way Jesus couched His request: "If it is possible." He left the answer to the Father when He said, "Yet not as I will, but as you will." Although Jesus keenly sensed the bitter suffering He was to undergo, He freely subjugated His desire to the Father. He based His own willingness upon the Father's will.

4. *What was the answer to Jesus' prayer?* His answer was that the will of the Father would be done. The cup did not pass from Him, for He withdrew the petition in deference to His Father's will. But He got an answer to His prayer. Jesus was strengthened for the mission He had come to fulfill when an angel from heaven appeared to Him and strengthened Him (Luke 22:43).

As leaders, doing the right thing for the right reasons might require you to drink the bitter cup in form of ridicule, rejection, and anger.

Your human tendency will be to try to avoid the pain. Leading like Jesus will call you to proceed in faith and to trust in God's grace to provide you with the courage to do the right thing and finish the task.

The Power of Preemptive Prayer

In leading like Jesus, prayer should never be relegated to our last resort in times of deep distress. It is our most powerful, most immediately accessible, most useful resource for responding to the moment-to-moment challenges of both good and bad times. That's why preemptive prayer is important.

Phil has written the following poem, which shows the possibilities of prayer:

Just Suppose

Just suppose, when I pray, there really is someone listening who cares about me and wants to know what is on my mind.

Just suppose, when I pray, it changes me and my view of how the universe operates and who is involved.

Just suppose, I put my doubts aside for a minute and consider the possibility that someone who knew me before I was born loves me, warts and all, without condition or reservation, no matter how badly I have behaved in the past.

Just suppose, a prayer was my first response instead of my last resort when facing a new challenge or an old temptation.

Just suppose, I lived each day, knowing that there is an inexhaustible supply of love for me to pass along to others.

Just suppose.

In chapter 4, we described the four stages of a learner and how a leader as teacher must appropriately respond to help a follower move to the next learning stage. We spoke of the leader-follower/teacher-learner relationship being a partnership and how each member of that partnership needs to take time to identify his own potential pride and fear issues to avoid the EGO factor stifling their relationships.

When that time of honest reflection reveals a problem to be faced, prayer is the most powerful first step to bringing God's promises into the equation. Philippians 4:6–7 tells us,

> Do not be anxious about anything, but in everything, by prayer and petition, with thanksgiving, present your requests to God. And the peace of God, which transcends all understanding will guard your hearts and your minds in Christ Jesus.

As you look forward to the work of the day, you will probably find that you are acting as a leader in some situations and as a follower in others. You will also find that you may be dealing with varying stages of learning, both yours and that of the people with whom you are working. For instance, you may be called on to play the role of a coach to a group of seasoned people—masters at what they do—who have lost their enthusiasm for an important but routine task, yet at the same time, you may play the role of a novice learning a new computer system from someone three levels down from you in an organization. Both roles will have EGO challenges, and both are opportunities to serve. Each can be subject to the energizing power of preemptive prayer. It might be a good idea to transform today's to-do list into today's prayer list and let God into the picture.

In chapter 7, you will find a series of prayers and devotions that speak to the particular EGO temptations associated with each stage of development and each leadership role you may face as a leader and as a follower/learner.

The ACTS Method of Prayer

People often ask us how to pray. First of all, prayer is not a technique; it is essentially a conversation with God. We all need to develop our own style of conversing with the Father. For those of you who would like a framework to get started, let us suggest ACTS as a way to begin. This simple acronym—ACTS—can help you remember your four basic parts of prayer. It has helped many beginners in prayer and served as a compass for weather-beaten veterans. Try it for a few days.

Adoration. All prayer should begin here. Tell the Lord that you love Him and appreciate Him for who He is. "Yours, O Lord, is the greatness and power and the glory and the majesty and the splendor, for everything in heaven and earth is yours. Yours, O Lord, is the kingdom; you are exalted as head over all" (1 Chronicles 29:11).

Confession. Immediately when we come into the presence of a holy God, we sense our inadequacies and are convicted that we all fall short of God's glory. Therefore, our first response to meeting and adoring God is confession. Sometimes we have to confess our sins even before we express our adoration and love. "If we confess our sins, he is faithful and just and will forgive us our sins and purify us from all unrighteousness" (1 John 1:9).

Thanksgiving. Thanksgiving is the heartfelt expression of gratitude to God for all He has done in creation, in redemption, and in our lives. During this part of the prayer, thank God specifically for all that He has done for you since the last time you talked. As the old hymn says,

"Count your blessings, name them one by one. Count your many blessings; see what God has done." What if tomorrow you only had the things that you thanked God for today? Toothpaste, air, water, clothes, family, job . . . you name it. Heed the scripture: "Sing and make music in your heart to the Lord, always giving thanks to God the Father for everything, in the name of our Lord Jesus Christ" (Ephesians 5:19–20).

Supplication. Finally, we get to the part of prayer where most of us start—asking. *Supplication* is just a big word for asking for what you need. Start by praying about others' needs and then ask for your own needs to be met. It's OK to have a big "wish list." According to God's Word, we can ask with confidence. "Ask and it will be given you; seek and you will find; knock and the door will be opened to you" (Matthew 7:7).

Pause and Reflect

One of the most revealing questions you could ask a leadership candidate is "How is your prayer life?" The answer will speak volumes about where and how the leader might lead. Here's a question for you: "How is *your* prayer life?"

The Habit of Dwelling in the Word

If you only use the Bible to study and apply its practical wisdom about dealing with people and overcoming internal challenges, it still would stand alone as the greatest book ever written. But the Bible is so much more than a how-to manual for dealing with people; it is an intimate love letter written to you from your Father. As someone once told us, the BIBLE stands for **B**asic **I**nstructions **B**efore **L**eaving **E**arth.

Through the words of Scripture, God invites you daily to experience new and exciting dimensions of His love. Scripture is the holy

Word from the holy God, delivered by holy men, to teach holy truths and to make people holy. "All Scripture is God breathed and is useful for teaching, rebuking, correcting and training in righteousness, so that the man of God may be thoroughly equipped for every good work" (2 Timothy 3:16–17).

It is well and good to know that the Bible is useful, reliable, and valuable. It is another thing to make it your own in a practical way. It is only profitable if you read it. How can you make the Word of God more effective in your life as a leader?

There are five practical ways you can cultivate the habit of studying Scripture—hearing, reading, studying, memorizing, and meditating. You may already know these steps, but are you practicing them? If not, it will take some time for them to become a habit.

Pause and Reflect

After each of the following explanations, evaluate where you are with your own practical application, what you plan to do to make it a habit, and what deadline you will set as a target for each one to become a Scripture habit.

Give yourself time to add one discipline to another until all are part of your habits of dwelling in the Word. You are in the process of becoming a servant leader and leading like Jesus for life, and it will be better for you to master these Scripture habits one at a time, beginning with the one that most appeals to you. Then you can add another on your own schedule.

Hear the Word

The simplest way to receive the Word is to hear it from someone else. Even a child or a person who cannot read can hear the Bible. "If anyone has ears to hear, let him hear" (Mark 4:23). "Faith comes from hearing the message, and the message is heard through the word of Christ" (Romans 10:17).

The parable of the sower, found in Matthew 13:3–23, lists four kinds of hearers of the Word: the *apathetic hearer* hears the Word but is not prepared to receive and understand it (v. 19); the *superficial hearer* receives the Word temporarily but does not let it take root in the heart (v. 20–21); the *preoccupied hearer* receives the Word but lets the worries of this world and the desire for other things choke it out (v. 22); and the *reproducing hearer* receives the Word, understands it, bears fruit, and brings forth results (v. 23). Which kind of hearer are you?

Here are four examples of resources for hearing the Word:

1. Sermons in church, on the radio, CDs, or tapes
2. *The NIV Audio Bible*, which dramatizes the reading of God's Word[2]
3. *The Visual Bible* DVDs, which dramatize the New International Version of selected books[3]
4. *Following Jesus: Making Disciples of Oral Learners*—more than four hundred Bible stories told orally[4]

However you choose to hear the Word, if you don't find a way to capture it, you will soon forget. For example, can you remember what was said the last time you heard the Word or a sermon?

Pause and Reflect

One way to apply what you hear is to ask yourself the following questions and jot down the answers. You might want to record them in your personal journal or make a form to help you remember.

- What did God say to me through this message?
- How does my life measure up to this Word?
- What actions will I take to line up my life with this Word?
- What truth do I need to study further?
- What truth can I share with another person?

Read the Word

The second way you learn God's Word is to read it. "Blessed is the one who reads the words of this prophecy, and blessed are those who hear it and take to heart what is written in it, because the time is near" (Revelation 1:3). Here are a few suggestions on how to read the Word.

Allow enough time to read the Word reflectively. God told Joshua, "Meditate on it day and night, so that you may be careful to do everything written in it. Then you will be prosperous and successful" (Joshua 1:8).

Do not read too much Scripture at one time. If you read too much Scripture at once, you cannot meditate on its meaning and let God speak directly to you and your situation. Start with something manageable, like these verses from Psalm 103: "Praise the Lord, O my soul; all my inmost being, praise his holy name. Praise the Lord, O my soul, and forget not all his benefits" (vv. 1–2).

Balance your reading of the Word. Jesus said, "'Everything must be fulfilled that is written about me in the *Law of* Moses, the *Prophets*, and the *Psalms*.' Then he opened their minds so they could understand the

Scriptures" (Luke 24:44–45, emphasis added). These three designations of Scripture cover all the counsel of God that will be available to you. You may read the Bible from Genesis to Revelation over a year by reading three chapters a day and five on Sunday. Another plan is to read a chapter from the Old Testament and a chapter from the New Testament each day. Or you might prefer to read through a book of the Bible one chapter a day before moving to another book.

Apply the Word to your life each day. To take it to heart, ask God to show you what His Word means to you and for your life. Jesus promised, "If you obey my commands, you will remain in my love, just as I have obeyed my Father's commands and remain in his love" (John 15:10).

Every time you apply the Word of God to your life, you grow closer to Him. Every time you fail to apply it, you leave the Word, like scattered seed, beside the road where Satan can steal it. Once you have heard His Word, you are prepared to respond to it in prayer and obedience. Jesus said, "If anyone loves me, he will obey my teaching, my Father will love him, and we will come to him and make our home with him" (John 14:23).

Study the Word

When you study the Word, you go deeper into its meaning and application. "Now the Bereans were of more noble character than the Thessalonians; for they received the message with great eagerness and examined the Scriptures every day to see if what Paul said was true" (Acts 17:11).

With study, you begin to have more power in your handling of the Word. Bible study is an in-depth look into the Scripture, to learn and discover more than you would see during a simple overview or in a devotional reading. Study involves comparing what the Bible says in one passage to other passages throughout the Bible. It might begin with a question that prompts you to search the Bible for its answer. It often includes gaining additional information through commentaries and study helps.

Memorize the Word

A deeper way to get the Word into your heart is to memorize it. When you remember the Word, it really lives in you, you live in it, and God's promises become your possessions. "How can a young man keep his way pure? By living according to your word. . . . I have hidden your word in my heart that I might not sin against you" (Psalm 119:9, 11).

There are several reasons to memorize Scripture. In the account of Christ's temptation in the wilderness (Matthew 4:1–11), Jesus set the example. He used Scripture as the sword of the Spirit against Satan, even when Satan tried to misuse Scripture as a part of the temptation. Memorizing scriptures helps you gain victory over sin. It also helps you answer when people have questions about your faith. "Always be prepared to give an answer to everyone who asks you to give the reason for the hope you have" (1 Peter 3:15). Being able to recite scriptures by heart helps you to meditate on it and gives you direction for your daily life at any moment. Most of all, the greatest benefit of memorizing scriptures comes from obedience to doing what God commands. "These commands that I give you today are to be upon your hearts" (Deuteronomy 6:6).

The president of the Lead Like Jesus ministry, Phyllis Hendry, shared with us her personal testimony of how memorizing scriptures has helped her lead like Jesus. When she was eight, a group came to her school and offered the students in her class a chance to go to a two-week summer camp—with swimming pools, tennis courts, and many other fun things to do—for free! All the students had to do was memorize three hundred Scripture verses.

Young Phyllis was up to the challenge, so she committed to memorizing those scriptures. She got up at 6:00 a.m. each day, memorized a verse, and then recited it to her father before school. Every morning, her father would pray, "Lord, help her remember these scriptures, and plant them as seeds in her heart." At the end of each week, she would recite all seven verses for her father, who would sign a form to verify that she had memorized them.

By the end of the school year, Phyllis had memorized all three hundred verses and earned a free admission to the two-week summer camp. But there were two things she had not considered. First, she had never been away from her parents for two entire weeks. Second, no one else in her class had taken the challenge to memorize the verses, so she didn't know anyone at camp!

By Wednesday of the first week of camp, Phyllis called home in tears and begged her mom to come get her. Her mom reminded her how hard she had worked for the entire year to get to this camp and persuaded Phyllis to stay until Saturday. She stayed, but she was miserable the entire time. When her parents came to pick her up on Saturday, Phyllis went home, disappointed because she had worked so hard but didn't enjoy her reward.

But she didn't realize at that time what her real reward was. The real reward of her commitment to memorize Scripture was what she learned. She didn't have to be afraid, because Isaiah 43:1 told her that God knew her by name, and she was His. She could call on God anytime, because Jeremiah 33:3 told her that God would answer her and tell her "great and unsearchable things." Ephesians 3:20 told her that God would do "immeasurably more" than anything she could "ask or imagine"—and she had a big imagination!

Phyllis never knew how those seeds would be planted in her heart until many years later, when her husband of twenty-two years collapsed from a heart attack. During the ambulance ride and in the hospital, Phyllis's mind was filled with the words of Jeremiah 29:11, a verse she had memorized as a child: "For I know the plans I have for you, plans to prosper you and not harm you, plans to give you a hope and a future."

When the doctor told Phyllis that her husband had passed away, somewhere in her head, Phyllis heard the words of 2 Corinthians 5:8 (KJV): "Absent from the body . . . present with the Lord," which assured her that her husband was in the presence of Jesus. Then she heard Proverbs 3:5–6: "Trust in the LORD with all your heart and lean not on your own understanding; in all your ways acknowledge him, and he will make your paths straight." And she was comforted by the words of Psalm 34:18: "The LORD is close to the brokenhearted."

The scriptures Phyllis memorized as a child have continued to bless her and bring her encouragement and comfort in the fifteen years since her husband passed away. Those verses have truly been seeds that were planted in her heart at an early age and have since taken deep root in her life.

How to Memorize Scripture[5]

1. Choose a verse that speaks to your need or that the Lord points out to you.
2. Understand the verse. Read it in context and in different translations.

3. Commit the verse to memory in your favorite translation. Divide it into natural, meaningful phrases and learn it word by word. If you learn it word-perfect in the beginning, it will be set in your memory, will be easier to review, will give you boldness when you are tempted, and will convince the person with whom you are sharing that he or she can trust your word. Memorize the reference and say it before and after the verse to fix it in your memory. Be ready if someone asks where it is in the Bible.
4. Develop some memory aids to help you remember the verse. For example, you might record it on a cassette tape, MP3, or CD so you can listen to it. Leave a long pause after each verse so you can practice quoting it. Then record the verse a second time so you can hear it again after you have quoted it without having to rewind it. Include the reference before and after.
5. Locate and underline the verse in your Bible so you can visualize it on the page.
6. Write the verse on a notecard or put it in your electronic organizer, including the Scripture reference and the topic it addresses. This allows you to relate the verse to a particular subject and enables you to find it when a need arises.
7. Place the written verse in prominent places so you can review it while you do other tasks. Put it over the kitchen sink, on the bathroom mirror, on your desk, on the dashboard of your car for reviewing at stoplights, or any place you will see it often.
8. Meditate on the verse, savoring each word. Say it over and over, emphasizing a different word each time. Turn the meaning around by adding the word *not* to the verse. This will help you see the positive truth in context.
9. Use these activities to set a verse in your mind: see it in pictorial

form; sing it making up your own tune; pray it back to God; practice it by making it a part of your life; and use it as often as possible.

10. Review, review, review. This is the most important secret of Scripture memorization. Review a new verse at least once a day for six weeks. Review the verse weekly for the next six weeks and then monthly for the rest of your life.
11. Have someone check your ability to quote the verse, or write the verse from memory and check it yourself.
12. Make Scripture memorization fun. Make a game of it. Get people to ask you any verse you have memorized at any time. This can be fun if a partner is also memorizing verses.

Meditate on the Word

Another way you live in the Word and the Word lives in you is to think about it or meditate on it. "His delight is in the law of the LORD, and on his law he meditates day and night" (Psalm 1:2–3).

While memorization puts God's Word in your head, meditation puts it in your heart. You meditate on God's Word when you focus on a specific verse of Scripture, concentrating on one verse a week. Select a verse that has been a key verse in a passage you have just read. Ask the Holy Spirit for His revelation as you meditate.

Here are some practical ways to meditate on God's Word:

1. Read the verses before and after to establish the theme and setting. These will aid you in interpretation. Then you may write a summary of the passage.
2. Write the verse(s) in your own words. Say your paraphrase aloud.
3. Read the verse over and over again, emphasizing a different word each time you repeat it. For example, in the verse "I can

do all things through Christ who strengthens me" (Philippians 4:13 KJV). First, emphasize the word "I," then the word "can," and so on, so that each word yields is full impact.

4. State the opposite meaning of the verse. For instance: "I cannot do anything if Christ does not strengthen me." What impact does the verse have now?
5. Write at least two important words from those you have emphasized in the verse. Ask these questions about the two words to relate the scripture to your needs: What? Why? Where? Who? How?
6. Personalize the verse: Let the Holy Spirit apply the verse to a need, a challenge, an opportunity, or a failure in your life. What will you do about this verse as it relates to your life? Be specific.
7. Pray the verse back to God. Put your own name or situation in the verse.
8. Refer to other passages that emphasize the truth of the verse. List thoughts or ideas you might not understand or might have difficulty applying in your life. Seek out instruction or help in these areas.
9. Write a way you can use the verse to help another person.

The Habit of Trusting in God's Unconditional Love

In seeking to lead like Jesus, we will come to points of decision that will reveal where we put our trust and hope. We will continue to face the fear of the negative consequences of taking a stand and the temptation to rely on our own self-accumulated resources and efforts as our source of self-worth and security.

We live in a world that fuels the fires of pride and fear. Through fads, fashion, and pressure to acquire more and better goods and services, we are constantly being lured into believing we can secure a sense of meaning and safety. Standing in absolute contrast to these temporary, always at-risk, never secure places to put our trust are the unconditional love and promises of God. Only in a relationship with God can we find and be assured of a never-ending supply of what we need to live and lead as Jesus would.

Accepting this reality is often a struggle between acknowledging God's promises as being general in nature and surrendering all your reservations that they are meant for you personally. Read the following promises of God and place your name where indicated:

> "For I am convinced that neither death nor life, neither angels nor demons, neither the present nor the future, nor any powers, neither height nor depth, nor anything else in all creation, will be able to separate [your name] from the love of God that is in Christ Jesus our Lord." (Romans 8:38–39)
>
> "Come to me, all you who are weary and burdened, and I will give you rest. Take my yoke upon you [your name] and learn from me, for I am gentle and humble in heart, and you will find rest for your souls. For my yoke is easy and my burden is light." (Matthew 11:28–30)
>
> "For God so loved [your name] that he gave his one and only Son, that whoever believes in him shall not perish but have eternal life." (John 3:16)

The implications of God's personal, unchanging, unrestrained love for you are enormous—so enormous that it might seem easier to consider

His love as so far beyond comprehension that you don't even try to understand it. If you do, you leave the dearly purchased gift unopened and the joy of the Giver unrealized.

The power of unconditional love is lived out in your relationships. For example, whenever we ask parents to raise their hands if they love their kids, all their hands go up. When we ask parents if they love their kids only if they're successful, all the hands eventually go down. You love your kids unconditionally, right?

If God's love for you was based on your performance to the standards that His righteousness requires, you would never have another moment free from anxiety. But what if you accept God's unconditional love for you? What if you admit that you can't earn enough, achieve enough, or control enough to get any more love? You already have all the love there is through Jesus! That is so powerful! Once you believe that you're perfectly, unconditionally loved, you won't get misled by earthly things.

A teenager once said to former missionary Avery Willis, "I am afraid that if I really surrender to God that He will send me to Africa as a missionary." Avery replied, "If someone says they will do anything you ask, would you punish them by making them do what they did not want to do? God loves you and He will only ask you to do what is for His glory and your good. Now He might have to change your heart so you are willing. Ask any missionary in Africa and he or she will tell you they are happier in the middle of God's love in Africa than they would be anywhere else in the world."

To Lead Like Jesus, You Must Love Jesus

Everything that you attempt in trying to lead like Jesus hangs in the balance of your response to the question that Jesus asked Peter: "Do you love Me?" Your answer should not be given lightly because Jesus will take it seriously. Your answer will reveal your true motivations for all you have done. Like Peter, all of us have given Jesus good reason to doubt our sincerity. We all fall short—sometimes in soul-shaming ways that we can hardly admit to ourselves, let alone to the One we have failed.

Do you love God enough to love His lost sheep? Jesus had a right to suspect Peter's love after his denial at His trial. Jesus always has the right to ask the question, "Do you *love* Me?" He did not ask Peter if he feared Him, respected Him, or admired Him; instead, He asked, "Do you *love* Me?" Jesus wants to see evidence that you love Him. Jesus said, "Inasmuch as you have done it to one of the least of these, you have done it unto Me" (Matthew 25:40 KJV). Jesus says that how you treat other people is how you treat Him.

To Lead Like Jesus, You Must Love Like Jesus

If you do not really love Jesus, then you will not truly love the people you lead. Nothing but the love of Christ will compel you to go cheerfully through the difficulties and discouragements you experience as a leader. However, Christ's kind of love will make your work easier, and it will encourage those you lead to serve wholeheartedly.

As Margie Blanchard says, "The antidote for fear and pride is faith in God's unconditional love for us." The true servant leader is one who clearly understands unconditional love and puts it into practice every day. All individuals need to be heard; they need to be praised; they need to be encouraged; they need to be accepted. As a leader, you need to practice these expressions of love. Why? Because you express your love of Jesus by loving those He puts in your path.

Jesus said, "But I tell you who hear me: Love your enemies, do good to those who hate you, bless those who curse you, pray for those who mistreat you (Luke 6:27–28). At times, we have all probably said, "Lord, I just can't love that person." But over time you may have learned to change your response to, "Although I can't make myself love that person, I will give You full right to love that person through me. Do anything You want to do through me, and I will do it as if to you." We have discovered that if we let Jesus love others through us and do good things for them, we learn to love them too.

When you cast off your doubts and reservations about God's love and accept that you can't earn it, don't deserve it, and can't add to it or lose it, you can proceed in that reality to live and lead in confidence, humility, and true freedom.

Pause and Reflect

Think of a time when, beyond a shadow of doubt, you experienced God's love for you personally, specifically, and in a way that only He and you knew its true significance in your life. How did you feel at the time? How do you feel at this moment? What do you need to say to God?

The Habit of Intimate Community

Henri Nouwen once noted a consistent pattern in the daily life of Jesus that proceeded from solitude to community to service. The time Jesus spent in fellowship with His disciples seems to have been for their benefit and His.

Among the twelve that He called out to be His apostles, Jesus had a small group of three—Peter, James, and John—with whom He seemed to have a particularly close relationship. He took these three with Him to the Mount of Transfiguration, where He revealed to them, in confidence, the true nature of His being (Matthew 17:1–9). The same three men were present when Jesus raised the daughter of the synagogue leader from the dead (Mark 5:21–43).

The most poignant and instructive episode involving this inner circle of intimate friendships occurred on the night Jesus would be arrested and start His final journey to the cross. In Matthew 26:37–38, we read, "He took Peter and the two sons of Zebedee along with him, and he began to be sorrowful and troubled. Then he said to them, 'My soul is overwhelmed with sorrow to the point of death. Stay here and keep watch with me.'"

Leadership can be a lonely business filled with great amounts of soul-draining human interaction but little soul-filling intimacy. Without some safe-harbor relationships where we can lay down all the armor and weapons needed to face the world and relax in confidence and unguarded communion, we become vulnerable to two debilitating frames of mind and spirit—the victim and the martyr. Allowed to blossom into resentment or a self-justification for seeking EGO-soothing instant gratification, these twin demons have been the downfall of many a leader in every walk of life.

Jesus emphasized the importance of a sense of communion of spirit in His prayer for His followers to attain the joy that He had in unity and fellowship with His Father. Jesus told His disciples,

> As the Father has loved me, so have I loved you. Now remain in my love. . . . My command is this: Love each other as I have loved you. Greater love has no one than this that he lay down his life for his friends. You are my friends if you do what I command. I no longer

> call you servants. Because a servant does not know his master's business. Instead I call you friends; for everything that I learned from my Father I have made known to you. (John 15:9, 12–15)

When we rely on our own perspective of how we are doing, we are bound to slip into convenient rationalizations and blind spots that can quickly undermine our integrity and trust of those who look to us for leadership.

Truth-Tellers

We all need trusted truth-tellers, preferably those not directly impacted by what we do, who can help us keep on course. If you can't name any active truth-tellers in your life, or if you have avoided or undervalued the ones you have, it's time to change. Having truth-tellers is probably the greatest resource for growth that you can have. Ken's father used to tell him, "I learned in the navy if you don't hear about any problems, watch out, because you are about to go over the side. You have mutiny on your hands, because the people around you have cut you off from the truth."

Too often in organizations, self-serving leaders cut off feedback by killing the messenger. Eventually the leader is fired, and although people had been available who could have given him or her helpful information, these leaders cut off the opportunity to grow. Feedback is a gift. If somebody gives you a gift, what do you say to them? "Thank you." Then you ask more questions to understand what is being said and why, such as, "Where did you get it?" "Are there any special instructions to help me use it?" "Can you tell me more about it?" "Who else do I need to ask about it?"

Bring truth-tellers into your life, and they will tell you the truth if they know you'll listen. It doesn't mean you have to do everything that they say, but they want to be heard. And in the process if you'll share some of your vulnerability, then the give-and-take is fabulous. "Two are better than one, because they have a good return for their work: if one falls down, his friend can help him up. But pity the man who falls and has no one to help him up. . . . Though one may be overpowered, two can defend themselves. A cord of three strands is not quickly broken" (Ecclesiastes 4:9–10, 12). We encourage you to contact people and work out an accountability relationship with regular times of truth-telling.

Being open to feedback from other people is not the only way to grow. Being willing to disclose vulnerabilities to other people is another. We're all vulnerable. We all fall short. Don't be afraid to share your vulnerability. Being vulnerable is one of the most powerful things you can do to build a team and to build relationships with people you're leading. They know you're not perfect, so don't act as if you are. More times than not, they know your imperfections long before you reveal them.

Disclosing your vulnerabilities doesn't mean expressing all your inner thoughts. Rather, you want to share task-relevant information, struggles you are working on as a leader. If a truth-teller says you're not a good listener, then what a wonderful thing to come in front of the team and share that. For example, you might say, "Bill was kind enough to share feedback with me about my listening. I didn't realize that when you say things to me, I jump right on to my own agenda. But now I know and I would like to improve it, and the only way I can improve it is if you will help me." As Proverbs 27:6 says, "Wounds from a friend can be trusted, but an enemy multiplies kisses."

Small Group Accountability Fellowship

In *Leadership by the Book*, one of the central characters, Michael, explains how he got into trouble after a successful start at becoming a servant leader. Michael observes, "When I boil it down, it was a combination of ego and self-imposed isolation."[6]

Throughout His earthly ministry, Jesus had all kinds of relationships with all kinds of people, but He maintained a special, intimate relationship with a small group of disciples. To put things in perspective, Jesus had hundreds, or even thousands, of people flocking to Him everywhere He went. Dozens of men and women followed Him consistently from town to town. And yet He had twelve specially chosen disciples to whom He entrusted His mission, and three inner-circle confidantes—Peter, James, and John—to lean on in crucial times. All of us need someone, or several someones, who love us enough to still be our friend no matter what they learn about us.

In Mark 9:2–12, we are told that Jesus took Peter, James, and John with Him to a high mountain and revealed to them the full reality of His God-nature on the Mount of Transfiguration. There He instructed them to keep what they had observed in confidence. In Mark 14:33, Jesus again gathered the same three men to Himself as He approached the crucifixion. Jesus demonstrated how much He valued the fellowship of those who knew Him best by taking them into the inner circle of His suffering in Gethsemane. As we commit to becoming more like Jesus in our leadership service, it is vital that we don't miss the important example Christ provided on how to combat the loneliness and isolation that can often be a part of being a leader.

If you are to maintain and grow in your daily walk as a Jesus-like leader, you need similar relationships. The temptations and challenges to be an ego-driven and fear-motivated leader are going to continue and probably intensify. The value of having a safe-harbor relationship of support and accountability cannot be overemphasized. "Let us consider how we may spur one another on toward love and good deeds. Let us not give up meeting together. . . . But let us encourage one another" (Hebrews 10:24–25).

An Accountability Group Model

Purpose: To provide mutual support and accountability for continued growth and maturity in leadership as disciples of Jesus.

Group Size: Two to seven people, preferably all of the same sex.

Commitment: Six months of regular participation. The group will assess its effectiveness after six months and determine whether it should continue to meet.

Meeting Schedule: Weekly

Meeting Time Frame: 60 to 90 minutes

Agenda:

Opening prayer—5 minutes

Devotional prepared on a rotating basis by group members—20 minutes

Accountability questions processed—45 minutes

The group will mutually determine a maximum of *six* of the questions to be answered by each member at each meeting. These questions should reflect areas of importance to the individual efforts of the group to walk by faith on a daily basis as they lead like Jesus.

Ground Rules

1. All discussions are strictly confidential and are not to be shared with anyone outside the group.
2. Advice is given only as requested.
3. Members should not be pressed to be more specific about personal struggles than they feel comfortable in sharing with the group. No "open heart surgery" is to be performed by the group.

Sample Questions

1. Since our last meeting, have you maintained a daily habit of prayer and time in God's Word?
2. Have you treated your family, peers, co-workers, supervisors, and employees as objects of God's love?
3. Have you allowed your pride or fear to drive your leadership decisions?
4. Have you maintained a healthy balance between work, family, church, and personal time?
5. Have you compromised your integrity in any way?
6. Have you been anywhere this week that could be seen as compromise?
7. Have you exposed yourself to any sexually explicit material?
8. Have you trusted God's timing in your life?
9. Have you missed an opportunity to teach and grow others?
10. Have you fulfilled the demands of your calling this week?
11. Have you missed an opportunity to give an apology or forgive someone?
12. What sin has plagued you in your efforts to lead like Jesus since we met last?
13. Have you just lied in answering any of the above questions?

Pause and Reflect

Name the special people in your life who will love you enough to tell you what you need to hear. How are you improving that special relationship? What can you do to make sure it stays alive and well? Who needs you to hold them accountable? Do you love them enough to tell them what they need to know?

Practicing the Habits Gives You Peace

Peace may sound like a strange characteristic in a leader. However, Jesus, the Prince of Peace, exhibited it throughout His ministry. Peace is an attractive trait in a leader, and many leaders rise to power on promises of peace. Jesus demonstrated peace most when everything around Him seemed to be in conflict. People sense when a leader is in control of himself and have explicit faith in what he is doing.

What Decision Will You Make?

The world needs to see God, and the only way they will see Him is if they see God through us. Each of us has a decision to make: will we choose to lead like everyone else, or will we choose to lead like Jesus by practicing these five habits?

When former professional football player Rosey Grier spoke at our 2003 Lead Like Jesus Celebration, he shared a compelling personal example of the importance of deciding to lead like Jesus—and being prepared to do so by practicing these five habits:

You know what I wanted to do as a football player? I wanted to carry the ball! But they wouldn't let me carry the ball; I was too big. I played in five world championship games with the Giants, and then I got traded to the L.A. Rams. I wanted to carry the football, but they wouldn't let me carry the football. They put me on defense.

One day, we're in the Coliseum, and we're playing the Green Bay Packers. They drove from their five-yard line down to our five-yard line, so we called a time-out. Our guys huddled up and said, "They're going to score on us. What should we do?" Someone in the back said, "Let's run a blitz."

Now, they didn't know we were going to run a blitz. So the QB struts out and says, "Everybody go down!" Then Deacon Jones, Merlin Olsen, Lamar Lundy, and myself start coming after him. While he was fading back with the ball, he closed his eyes. . . . Deacon Jones, Merlin, and Lamar jumped on him, and there was no place left for me to jump on him.

Then the football popped up, just like that. I'm looking up at that football. All my life I've been wanting to carry that football. I heard a voice in my head say, "You're supposed to yell out, 'Ball!'" Well, the week before, I had yelled out, "Ball!" and Merlin Olsen got the football and started running down the sideline. I was so mad, I caught up to him and said, "Say, Merlin, let me carry the football some." He said, "No, man, I'm carrying it all the way!" So I said, "Well, let me carry it for a little while and give it back to you." He said, "No way!" So I didn't block for him—and he didn't make it either. . . .

So here I'm standing, looking at that football, and I have to make a decision. I'm thinking, "I'm not going to say, 'Ball!' because

I want to run ninety-five yards for a touchdown myself." But as I'm standing there, with my hands up in the air, that old voice in my head says, "Can you catch?"

You know what, I had never practiced catching. When I had an opportunity to run ninety-five yards for a touchdown, I wasn't able to do it because I was not prepared.

Have you made the decision to lead like Jesus? If so, are you prepared? As followers of Christ, we are all part of the team, and we all have a part to play. Today is the day to make your decision. Will you decide to lead like Jesus? And will you choose to be prepared to run all the way to glory by putting into practice the five habits of servant leadership that He modeled?

Summary

- Jesus stayed on track with His mission by applying five key habits that countered the negative forces in His life:
    1. Solitude
    2. Prayer
    3. Study and application of Scripture
    4. Accepting and responding to God's unconditional love
    5. Involvement in supportive relationships
- Adopting these same habits is essential for those who seek to follow Jesus as their role model for leadership.

Chapter 6

WHY LEAD LIKE JESUS?

Now that you know about the *heart*, *head*, *hands*, and *habits* of leading like Jesus, you are aware, more than ever before, that being a Lead Like Jesus leader is all about changing what you think about and how you act as a leader. When you read the title of this chapter, you may have said to yourself, "Isn't it a little late to be talking about why we should lead like Jesus? Shouldn't that have been one of the first chapters?" Many others would agree with you. Why?

Whenever we are asked to do something different in life, the change agent—whether a manager, a spouse, a parent, a sibling, a colleague, or a friend—usually starts off by attempting to convince you of all the benefits of the change you are being asked to make. Yet it's been found that the benefits—the *impact* and the "why" of change—is the fourth-ranked concern people have during change.[1] People are first interested in *information concerns*. "Tell me what you have in mind. What is needed? What is wrong with the way things are now?" When you have information concerns, you don't want to be sold on the change; you simply want to understand it. Next, people are interested in *personal concerns*. "How will doing this affect me? Do I have what it takes to integrate the suggested change in my life?" Here, the focus is on the details involved in making the change a reality. Third, people have *implementation concerns*. "What do I do first, second, third, etc.?"

Throughout this book, we have been dealing with these three concerns. First, we gave you as much *information* as we can on what leading like Jesus is all about—the issues of the *heart*, *head*, *hands*, and *habits*. We also dealt with your *personal concerns* and fears about leading like Jesus in the *heart* chapter by showing you how, by Exalting God Only, to connect with the power behind the promises that Jesus gives to all who follow Him:

> "If God be for us, who can be against us?" (Romans 8:31)
>
> "The things which are impossible with men are possible with God." (Luke 18:27)
>
> "I can do all things through Christ who strengthens me." (Philippians 4:13)
>
> "I am the vine, you are the branches; he who abides in me and I in him, he bears much fruit. For apart from me, you can do nothing." (John 15:5)

In the *hands* and *habits* chapters, we focused on what you have to do behaviorally and habit-wise to implement a Lead Like Jesus philosophy.

In this chapter, we want to focus on the benefits or *impact concerns* you might have about this call to lead like Jesus. As we consider the benefits of leading like Jesus, we will discuss spiritual, practical, and legacy reasons for leading like Jesus.

Spiritual Reasons for Leading Like Jesus

The spiritual reasons for leading like Jesus are as compelling as they are challenging in a world where EGO-driven striving for self-gratification, self-promotion, and self-protection describe the way leadership is done at every level of human relationship.

As followers of Jesus, we must seek to lead like Jesus in this world. As a philosophy of leadership, servant leadership may be considered one option among many others; but as a theology of leadership, it is a mandate for all who call Jesus Lord. Foundational to tapping into the essence of leading like Jesus is embracing a life purpose of loving God and loving and serving people.

Servant Leaders Seek First the Kingdom

Leadership is primarily about two things—results and relationships. It is how we influence others to accomplish a specific mission, vision, and goal, whether grand and glorious or humble and mundane. Leading like Jesus is infusing harmony in our influence on other people with God's plan for their lives and ours. In Matthew 6:33, Jesus calls those who would follow Him not to worry about producing the results of most of their labors by telling them, "Seek first the kingdom of God and his righteousness, and all these things will be added to you."

As we journey together to consider the results and relationships sides of leading like Jesus, we will attempt to follow this same rank-order of priority. We encourage you to consider results and relationships as both lifelong goals of your leadership and as the answer to the underlying prayer of all you come in contact with—to be respected and guided in truth and ways that celebrate and develop their unique gifts to attain the highest good.

Pause and Reflect

Søren Kirkegaard once noted, "If you don't seek first the kingdom of God, you will never seek it." How do you intend to take this caution seriously as you seek to lead like Jesus?

Servant Leadership Honors God and His Commandments

When Jesus was asked what the greatest commandment was, He replied, "Love the Lord your God with all your heart and with all your soul and with all your mind. This is the first and greatest commandment. And the second is like it: 'love your neighbor as yourself'" (Matthew 22:37–39).

There is an old, yet still provocative question that each follower of Jesus can be held accountable to answer: "If being a Christian were a crime, would there be enough evidence in your life to convict you?" In other words, is what you say you believe making a significant difference in how you behave? Servant leadership is a concrete expression of a daily commitment to live out the Word of God and the will of God and thereby advance the kingdom of God.

Pause and Reflect

What three pieces of evidence would you rely on as your commitment to lead like Jesus? Is it hard evidence or merely circumstantial?

Servant Leadership Puts the Love of Jesus into Action

As we have considered what it means to lead like Jesus, we have sought to illuminate some of the secrets of servant leadership by observing the One who lived it to perfection—Jesus. We have sought wisdom and insights from His preparation and His leadership effectiveness and commitment. We have extracted key lessons in how to balance results and people in fulfilling our common and individual missions as modern-day disciples of Jesus.

The overarching truth about leading like Jesus is that it can only be accomplished by continuing to walk closer and closer to Him in a surrendered relationship of trust and love. It is in and through this narrow gate that all who want to lead like Jesus must travel—belief in His abiding love and accepting the call to follow Him. As we have said, leading like Jesus is, at its essence, learning to love like Jesus.

When Jesus restored Peter to the leadership role he was to play among His followers, Jesus had only one qualifying question: "Do you truly love me?" (John 21:15). The theme of Jesus' instruction was "Feed my lambs. . . . Take care of my sheep. . . . Feed my sheep" (vv. 15–17).

Ours is a love relationship with our heavenly Father. It is grounded in His unconditional love for us as expressed through His Son. It is one in which we are called to love one another—our neighbors, our enemies. To lead like Jesus is always to seek to do the loving thing in the use of our influence on the thinking, behavior, and development of others.

This may seem an impossible, impractical standard to adopt in lives lived in constant motion and never-ending value choices we need to make every day. But that is exactly what we are called to do!

Even if we overcome the demons of pride and fear in seeking to serve rather than be served, we are still left with the question: "What is the most loving thing I can do in this leadership moment as I seek to lead like Jesus?" Doing the loving thing as a leadership principle requires wisdom, patience, courage, sacrifice, and hard work. But if we can't describe it in behavioral terms, we won't be able to measure our success and failures in a meaningful way.

At the behavioral level, the loving thing will swing widely from acting and speaking, to refraining from acting and remaining silent. At the level of intention, it should remain the ever-present constant. Jesus provided us with a vast treasure of example of what it means to do the loving thing as a leader.

Consider the following: Jesus healed with a touch. He comforted with a word. He fed the hungry. He counseled the mistaken and the downhearted. He mourned with the grieving. He calmed the terrified. He confronted falsehood and spoke the truth. He listened with compassion and discernment. He took time with the weak and powerless. He went to the cross for us all.

In his *Commentary on the Epistle to the Galatians*, fourth-century church historian Jerome wrote this about the apostle John: "When he tarried at Ephesus to extreme old age, and could only with difficulty be carried to the church in the arms of his disciples, and was unable to give utterance to many words, he used to say no more at their several meetings than this, '*Little children, love one another.*' At length the disciples and fathers who were there, wearied with always hearing the same words, said, 'Master, why dost thou always say this?' 'It is the Lord's command,' was his worthy reply, 'and if this alone be done, it is enough.'"

Pause and Reflect

Think of a time when doing the loving thing instead of the popular thing, the easiest thing, the quickest thing, the most rewarding thing, or the safest thing would have restored or retained trust. Remember that moment for future reference.

Servant Leadership Models Jesus to Others

When Peter spoke to the next generation of church leaders, he urged them, "Serve—not because you must, but because you are willing, as God wants you to be; not greedy for money, but eager to serve; not lording it over those entrusted to you, but being examples to the flock" (1 Peter 5:2–3). At the beginning of the book, we noted that there was no plan B option given by Jesus to His first disciples or His modern-day ones regarding how they were to lead and serve one another. He surrendered Himself to the will of His Father to fully accomplish His unique role as the sacrificial lamb for the sins of the world and to be the perfect model to be reproduced in the lives of His followers as a witness to the whole world.

As we go about our daily lives in relationship with others, each choice we make to serve or be served takes on added significance if we remain sensitive and aware of who may be watching and who we claim to represent. We go in the name of Jesus.

Practical Reasons for Leading Like Jesus

From a practical point of view, servant leadership best serves the dual objectives of effective leadership—results and relationships. Consider some of the ways in which this applies.

Servant Leadership Provides Better Service

Organizations led by servant leaders are more likely to take better care of their relationships with customers and colleagues. Today, if you don't take care of your customers, somebody else is waiting, ready, and willing to do it. The only thing your competition can't duplicate is the relationship your people have with your customers. Under servant leadership, these relationships can really grow, because the people closest to the customer are given the power to soar like eagles rather than quack like ducks. Servant leaders realize good results are the applause you get for taking care of the customers and creating a motivating environment for your people.

Servant Leadership Provides Better Leadership

Organizations led by servant leaders are less likely to experience poor leadership. In studying bad leadership, Barbara Gellerman found seven different patterns, falling along a continuum ranging from ineffective to unethical leadership. Ineffective leadership does not get the job done because of incompetence, rigidity, lack of self-control, or callousness. As you have learned in studying how to lead like Jesus, rigidity, lack of self-control, or callousness are incompatible with being a servant leader. What about incompetence?

Servant leadership enables humility to overcome *incompetence.* Suppose someone who is not qualified accepts a leadership position. What will it take for this person to become effective and get the job done? This question was asked of Henry Blackaby, author of *Experiencing God*, at a Vision and Values conference sponsored by the Young Presidents Organization. Prior to this question, participants were talking with Henry and Ken about whether you needed to always check if you had the proper strengths to take a particular leadership position.

Henry's response was classic. In essence, he said,

> That's an interesting concept, but it's not biblically sound. Name for me one leader in the Bible whom the Lord called who was qualified! Every one of them, including Moses and Mary, claimed in one way or the other that they were the wrong person for the job. The reality is that the Lord never calls the qualified; He qualifies the called.

When Henry was asked what it meant to be called, he emphasized humility. If you have a teachable spirit and your EGO is out of the way, the Lord and others around you will qualify you. That's what we've said throughout this book—true servant leadership involves humble service. True servant leadership embraces a humble sincerity that brings out the best in leaders and those they serve. That's exactly what Jesus did.

As we emphasized earlier, Jim Collins supports this truth in his best-selling leadership book *Good to Great*. According to Collins, when things are going well for typical self-serving leaders, they look in the mirror, beat their chests, and tell themselves how good they are. When things go wrong, they look out the window and blame everyone else. Great leaders, on the other hand, are humble. When things go well, they look out the window and give everybody else the credit. When things go wrong, these servant leaders look in the mirror and ask, "What could I have done differently to allow these people to be as great as they could be?"[2]

Servant leaders have solid self-esteem. As a result, they are willing to admit when they have a weakness or need assistance. Put in positions over their heads, they are able to reach out to their people for help. Servant leaders are willing to admit when they have a weakness or need assistance. By reaching out to their people for help, they create environments where new ideas and new solutions emerge.

Ken had a beautiful example of this in his own company. Because of a leadership crisis, they needed his daughter, Debbie, to take over the sales department. The only sales experience she had was working at Nordstrom in the summer. When she had her first meeting with of all of her salespeople, she told them that she needed their help if she was going to be effective. She flew around the country, met with her team, found out what their needs were, and figured out how she could help them. Responding to her humility, the salespeople reached out to make sure she had the knowledge she needed to be effective. With Debbie at the helm, last year the sales department produced the highest sales in the history of the company, far exceeding its annual goal.

Unethical leadership, in contrast to ineffective leadership, is about right and wrong. "Unethical leadership can be effective leadership just as ineffective leadership can be ethical," Gellerman states. "But unethical leadership cannot make even the most basic claim to decency and good conduct, and so the leadership process is derailed."[3]

Servant leadership wards off *unethical behavior*. Under servant leadership, when the vision and values are clearly defined, ethical and moral dilemmas are less likely to emerge. Drea Zigarmi, senior author of *The Leader Within*, contends that a moral dilemma exists when there are no guidelines for decision making, forcing an individual to rely on his or her own values and beliefs. An ethical dilemma arises when the organization has clearly established guidelines for behavior, and the individual must consciously decide to go along with or violate those guidelines.[4]

People and organizations work more effectively if clear vision and values are established up front. Unethical leadership is often the result of the moral confusion created by the organization's lack of clearly established guidelines that a compelling vision provides. As we have said, that's exactly where servant leadership begins.

Is the problem confined to business? No! Being more ethical and values driven benefits our families, churches, our community organizations, and anywhere we influence others. Leading like Jesus is for everyone, everywhere.

Servant Leadership Closes the Gap Between Success and Significance

Bob Buford, in his book *Halftime*, describes how most people, later in life, want to move from success to significance—from getting to giving.[5] People and organizations led by servant leaders are more likely to function well in values-based environments where success and significance are available at all levels. Led to serve one another as well as a common vision, people in these environments tend to work honestly and ethically.

The problem with self-serving leaders is that they never get out of their own way. If they were focused on significance—generosity, service, and loving relationships—they'd be amazed at how much success would come their way. For example, Mother Teresa couldn't have cared less about accumulation of wealth, status, and recognition. Her life was focused on serving others. Yet what happened? Success came her way. When leaders focus on significance first, their emphasis is on their people. Through that emphasis, success and results will follow.

Lead Like Jesus servant leaders, who model their values in the way they treat their people, create environments where everyone can find significance in what they do and the vision they serve. Leaders who are passionate about creating a motivational experience for everyone who comes in contact with their organization—employees, customers, suppliers, or members of the same community—not only improve the quality of their life but will also produce "significant success."

Leadership Legacy Reasons for Leading Like Jesus

Whether you like it or not, you will leave a leadership legacy. Why? Because we all influence the thinking and behavior of other people in our organizational leadership and/or life role leadership positions.

Lee Ross relates the following story, which reminds us that the legacy we leave will be the leadership we live:

> A young pastor friend named Dan shared that his father had been very ill and had recently died. Dan's father had been a strong Christian who modeled a Jesus-like attitude and behaviors in all areas of his life. He shared the story that his father had contracted a fast-moving form of melanoma and was told that he only had about one month to live. Just a few days before his death, Dan's father asked to see Bob, his best friend for over twenty-five years. Although Dan's father had repeatedly shared Christ with his friend, Bob had never accepted Jesus as his Savior.
>
> When Bob arrived at the hospital, Dan's dad asked to speak with him alone. Dan's father once again shared how much God loved him and how Jesus had died on the cross for his sins. There in that hospital room, Bob bowed his head and asked Jesus to forgive him and take control of his life.
>
> The next day, Dan's father passed away, but that is not the end of the story. Before he died, Dan's father had made one last request.

He wanted Bob to be baptized as a part of his funeral service. What a legacy! Even at his funeral, this wonderful Christian man demonstrated his faith and his desire to lead others to know Jesus. He didn't care about the spotlight shining on his life or his accomplishments. He wanted everyone to see what God had done in Bob's life!

We share that story with you so that you will seriously examine the leadership legacy you might be leaving behind. How do you want to be remembered as a leader by the people at work, at home, in your church, and in your community? Leading like Jesus is not a course; it is a lifestyle. Making the development of people an equal partner with performance is a decision you make. It is following the example of Jesus as a servant leader and pouring your life into the lives of other people. It is about leaving a leadership legacy of service.

Leaving a positive Lead Like Jesus legacy is not without challenges. We will look at four challenges and suggest ways that you can overcome these challenges to develop the servant leadership lifestyle of Jesus.

Remember, It's Not About You!

"When the hour came, Jesus and his apostles reclined at the table. . . . Also a dispute arose among them as to which of them was considered to be the greatest" (Luke 22:14, 24). Seating arrangements at a Jewish feast were very important. The host would always take the middle seat at the table. On the right side of the host would sit the first guest of honor, on the left side the second guest of honor; on the second right side would sit the third guest of honor, and so forth.

It seems that the disciples spent much time worrying about their position at dinner and in the kingdom of God. Scripture tells us that this dispute had been going on among the disciples for some time. Apparently, the disciples had a hard time hearing Jesus' message about leadership being first an act of service: "The greatest among you should be like the youngest, and the one who rules like one who serves" (Luke 22:26). Jesus wanted the disciples to understand that following Him was not about position; it was about service. The disciples did not fully understand this until Pentecost.

The first challenge for a Lead Like Jesus leader is to recognize that *it is not about you*. Your leadership is not about your position or your title or the amount of money you make; it is about following the servant leadership example of Jesus. The disciples were slow to understand this, and many leaders today do not understand this either! As you decide to lead like Jesus, remember this: "It is not about you." What God wants is what really matters.

Live Your Life with God-Grounded Confidence

In John 13:3, we read, "Jesus knew that . . . he had come from God and was returning to God." It is interesting that John makes this statement just before Jesus washes the feet of the disciples. Jesus "knew that He had come from God." What does this tell us? We believe it reminds us of the two key questions all Lead Like Jesus leaders must ask themselves: "Whose are you?" and "Who are you?"

At the very beginning of His ministry, Jesus clearly answered these two questions in the wilderness. There was no doubt in the mind of Jesus that He belonged to His Father and that His Father had sent Him to accomplish a very clear purpose. Because Jesus had settled these critical questions, He was able, without hesitation, to take on the role of the servant and wash the feet of the disciples. He was confident in the unconditional love that His Father had for Him and in the role He had been given.

The second challenge for a Lead Like Jesus leader is to develop a God-grounded confidence, as we discussed in chapter 2. Many leaders we know today are some of the most insecure people we have ever met. Out of a sense of insecurity and fear, they have not addressed these key issues in their lives, yet they try to lead at home, at work, and at church. This will only lead to disaster for the leader. As one author puts it, "All insecurity is rooted in an inadequate sense of belonging to God."[6]

Jesus clearly knew who He belonged to! Just as Jesus knew where He had come from and therefore could wash the feet of the disciples, you also must determine "whose you are" and "who you are" if you are going to confidently serve the people you are leading. John says Jesus knew he was "returning to God." In other words, Jesus knew His destination. He knew that after the crucifixion and resurrection, He would be with His Father in heaven.

Live a Life Full of Integrity

"He got up from the meal, took off His outer clothing, and wrapped a towel around His waist. After that, He poured water into a basin and began to wash His disciples' feet, drying them with the towel that was wrapped around Him" (John 13:4–5). Integrity means not only talking about being a Lead Like Jesus leader, but actually living it! Jesus had taught the disciples many times that leadership was about serving, not about position. In this scripture, we see that Jesus not only talked about serving, but He actually did it! He got down on His hands and knees and washed the dirty feet of the disciples.

One of the problems we see in the lives of leaders today is that they love to tell everyone else how they should serve and act, yet when it comes to their lives, they do not practice what they are preaching. Or as we like to say, they "stumble the mumble." Too often there is a real disconnect between what the leader says and what the leader does.

We believe that the next great movement in Christianity will be demonstration. If we want people to be interested in our faith in the future, we as Christians must practice what we preach. In other words, people need to not only hear Christian leaders talking about the message of Christ, but they need to see us living out this message in the way we lead and serve others.

Submit to the Will of God for Your Life

> When He had finished washing their feet, He put on His clothes and returned to His place. "Do you understand what I have done for you?" He asked them. "You call me 'Teacher' and 'Lord' and rightly so, for that is what I am. Now that I, your Lord and Teacher, have washed your feet, you also should wash one another's feet. I have set for you an example that you should do as I have done for you. I tell you the truth, no servant is greater than his master, nor is a messenger greater than the one who sent him. Now that you know these things, you will be blessed if you do them." (John 13:12–17)

After washing the feet of the disciples, Jesus asks them, "Do you understand what I have done for you?" This is a very important question as we come to the close of this book. Do you understand what Jesus has done for you? He has set the example of how you should live, and of how you should invest your life into the lives of the people you lead.

In verse 17, Jesus challenges His disciples: now that they understand, are they ready to do what He says? Are they ready to submit to His way of leading?

You have a variety of resources available if you have a leadership question or concern, but what we believe Jesus is challenging us to do is first to submit to His will for our lives as leaders. Jesus should be the first resource we go to if we have a leadership question. What's the problem? Jesus is the answer. Why? Because we have made a decision to submit our will to the will of God for our lives!

The issue is not just about commitment, but about submission. Henry Blackaby, in his book *Spiritual Leadership*, says, "Some spiritual leaders try to be more committed. What they need is to be more submitted."[7] In your spiritual life, you must first be willing to submit your life to God. This is the first and most important decision you will ever make. Have you submitted your entire life to God? Have you asked Jesus to forgive you of your sins? If not, you can do it right now! This is the first decision you must make if you are going to lead like Jesus.

The next part of this decision is submitting your life to God and letting Him control every aspect of your life, including your leadership responsibilities. When Jesus said, "You will be blessed if you do them (John 13:17)," He meant it. This is a promise He gives to those who choose to follow His example of servant leadership. Submission to the will of God for our lives as leaders will mean the blessing of eternal life with Him, and our lives will be a blessing to the lives of the people we have the privilege of leading! We will leave a positive leadership legacy.

Pause and Reflect

What four words best describe what you would hope to leave as your leadership legacy? Which ones are most in need of a new focus to become a reality?

Leading Like Jesus Begins with You

The fourth concern people have when they are asked to change how they are thinking and behaving is *collaboration*. Once you have information about what you are being asked to do, your *personal* and *implementation* concerns have been answered and you understand the "why" or *impact* of behaving differently, then your attention turns to collaboration. Who else do you want to involve or share with about your learning and desired change?

Before sharing your commitment to lead like Jesus with others, you first have to stay focused on your thoughts, actions, and behavior. That's what others will observe.You have taken the first step of an exciting new journey to lead like Jesus by reading this book. In the initial stages, as you begin to apply what you have learned at work, at home, or in the community, the landscape will look familiar. The people you are interacting with and working with will more than likely be the same people you interacted with and worked with before you started. Expect them to behave just as they have in the past and respond to your leadership as they always have. Even as they sense a change in how you are treating them, they will, at times, continue to question your motivations, misinterpret what you are trying to accomplish, and test your commitment. Some will embrace the change you seek to create, some will be skeptical, some will feel threatened by you, and some will oppose change for their own purposes.

It is important to realize that they have been conditioned to respond to you in a particular way. They will continue to respond this way until they sense your commitment is for the long haul and trust in their own ability to succeed. The longer you demonstrate a Lead Like Jesus servant leadership, the more people will change. As they embrace these principles, your workgroup, family, or community organization will change as well.

Don't make the mistake of first trying to change other leaders with whom you work. Focus on yourself. *Be the change you want to see in others*.

The roles and responsibilities in your life and the problems you face probably have not changed since you started reading this book. What has changed is how you approach them. Hard choices between self-serving and servant leadership decisions are bound to occur at as rapid a pace as before. People will continue to tempt you to use your time in good ways, but not the best ways.

Praise progress as you stand for your own operating values, and resist the temptation to edge God out of His rightful place as the audience of One in your life. You will find that it becomes easier to stand up for what is right after you do it for the first time and feel the joy of giving honor to the One you follow.

If you have an open organizational or life role leadership environment, you can start to teach what you have learned about leading like Jesus right away. As we have said, the best way to learn something is to teach it.

Leading like Jesus is responding to a monumental challenge to be lived out minute by minute in big and small decisions. It cannot be done perfectly, and trying to do so should not be the goal. But it can be the constant direction and ideal that we pursue without ceasing. In doing so, we will honor God along the way.

This involves going public with your good intentions. It could happen unexpectedly, when someone notices something different in the way you are leading and asks you, "What is going on?" Will you be prepared to respond?

The Bible calls us each to have a ready answer at a moment's notice:

> But in your hearts set apart Christ as Lord. Always be prepared to give an answer to everyone who asks you to give the reason for the hope that you have. But do this with gentleness and respect, keeping a clear conscience, so that those who speak maliciously against your good behavior in Christ may be ashamed of their slander. (1 Peter 3:15–16)

Or you may go public intentionally, as a declared beginning of a new or reconfirmed direction. As Joshua 24:14–15 says, "Fear the LORD and serve him with all faithfulness. . . . If serving the LORD seems undesirable to you, then choose for yourselves this day whom you will serve. . . . As for me and my household, we will serve the LORD."

Your Personal Leadership Statement

Imagine you're standing on a stage in front of an auditorium filled with the people you live and work with every day. The house lights are up. You can clearly see your spouse, your children and grandchildren, your brothers and sisters, your parents, your friends, your boss, your co-workers, the people you supervise, your pastor, and your neighbors.

Take a moment and picture each of their faces, looking up at you. All eyes and hearts are opened and focused on you and what you are about to say. There is love and anticipation in the air. This is the most positive crowd you can imagine standing in front of to deliver a message of vital importance to you and to them.

There is one feature of the room that commands your attention as you begin. On the wall immediately behind the audience is a cross.

Imagine taking a slight step forward and coming even closer to the smiling eyes and faces of these very special people as you begin to speak. You have taken special care in preparing what you are going to say and have written it down to be sure not to forget an important point. Imagine taking your written statement from your pocket and beginning to read your own personal statement of intent—leading people at a higher level. What would you say? Perhaps it would go something like this:

> Thank you all for coming to share this important moment with me. At one time or another, I have attempted to influence the thinking, actions, or development of each person in this room in their personal or professional life. In other words, I have sought to lead you somewhere for some purpose. This may have been in a formal way when we were acting out our roles in an organization or informally as part of our life role relationships.
>
> As a result, we have shared some successes together that left us both feeling good about what was accomplished and our relationship. Other times, we have shared frustration with both the results

and the impact on our relationship. For the times I have led you poorly, out of pride, fear, weariness, or just bad judgment, I apologize and ask for your forgiveness.

Without dismissing or minimizing the price we mutually paid for my past mistakes, I want today to ask each of you to help me by holding me accountable for leading at a higher level in the future. I have come to the personal conclusion that to make the most of the influence that has been entrusted to me, I need a trustworthy and relevant leadership role model to follow—one that will inspire and equip me to fulfill my life purpose in relationship to other people; one that allows me to live and lead a simplified life as the whole person God intended me to be and bring joy into the work and purpose of all my relationships.

As the old hymn says, "I have decided to follow Jesus. No turning back, no turning back." It is my heart's desire and commitment to seek to follow the leadership teachings and model of Jesus in all future opportunities I have to influence the thinking, behavior, and development of people. This means that I intend to be a servant leader. As Jesus said, "Just as the Son of Man did not come to be served but to serve" (Matthew 20:28), I now recognize that leadership is not all about me. It's about you, our mission, and the people we serve. Going forward, I want to serve rather than to be served.

Knowing me as you do, this probably sounds like an impossible goal to achieve, as it does to me in stating it as my intention. If perfection were my goal, it would be impossible to attain. If interrupted progress without relapses was what I was promising to deliver, you would be right to dismiss my intentions as nice but nothing to invest any hope in seeing put into practice. But what I am intending to do is to start each day seeking to make the best leadership decisions I can with the guidance of the Holy Spirit and to serve the highest purpose for the highest good in all my leadership decisions.

As it has been said, "Every journey begins with a first step." My first step in seeking to be a better leader will be taking time to listen—to listen to God, to our common mission and values, to you, and to the best of what the Scriptures and my heart and mind will reveal about leading like Jesus.

Pause and Reflect

If this isn't the speech you would give, what parts would you change and why? When you have it right, will you deliver it—if not to a collected audience, how about moment by moment in the leadership decisions you make?

If your organizational culture does not easily let you talk about Jesus, don't worry. Just behave as He did and become a great servant leader. Then when people are attracted to the way you lead and they ask you about it, you are free to share with them whom you follow. When people look at you, let them see Jesus. If they like what they see, then they will want to know where that came from; they are ready to learn and are good candidates for your speech.

In the final chapter, we give you the next steps to take as a Lead Like Jesus leader. It will provide you with tools and techniques that will help you behave on your good intentions. It is also our hope that this final chapter will provide you with ideas to *refine* and develop new and better ways for you to lead like Jesus.

Summary

- When people are asked to change, as we have been asking you to do to lead like Jesus, the rank-ordered concerns people have are: *information*, *personal*, *implementation*, *impact*, *collaboration*, and *refinement*.
- There are spiritual, practical, and leadership legacy benefits for leading like Jesus.
- From a spiritual point of view, servant leadership honors God and His commandments, puts the love of Jesus into action, and models Jesus to others.
- From a practical point of view, servant leadership provides better service, provides better leadership, and closes the gap between success and significance.
- Leading like Jesus can only be accomplished by continuing to walk closer and closer to Him in a surrendered relationship of trust and love. When you do that, you will leave a positive leadership legacy.

Chapter 7

NEXT STEPS TO LEAD LIKE JESUS

Leading like Jesus is a daily journey and challenge rather than a final destination. It can be done only in and through the power of the Holy Spirit in your life and committed relationships, first with God and then with others. The journey of leading like Jesus will always be filled with failures, roughly right behaviors, and out-and-out victories. Staying the course means frequently checking where you are and where you are headed and making necessary course corrections. The following tools are provided for your use on your Lead Like Jesus journey.

Tool #1 – Lead Like Jesus Readiness Exam

Primary Use

To remind you of the issues that matter most about your leadership activities

Instructions

Imagine you are sitting down with Jesus just before He sends you off to represent His kingdom, today, where you work and in all your personal relationships. Here are some questions Jesus might ask to make sure you are ready for the job.

Questions of the Heart

- Do you love Me?
- Do you trust Me?
- Will you serve Me by serving others?
- Do you believe that I will always love you regardless of your performance or the opinion of others?
- Are you willing to set aside instant gratification, recognition, and power to honor Me by doing the right thing?

Question of the Head

- Do you see your leadership as a season of service and stewardship?
- Do you have a compelling vision to lead your organization and a strategy to serve and help your people live according to that vision?

Questions of the Hands

- Are you willing to seek to understand by listening and sorting what you hear with service in mind rather than self?
- Are you willing to lead and learn from people who are different, think differently, look differently, and are older or younger than you?
- Are you willing to honor all work honestly performed as sacred?
- Are you ready to admit when you make a mistake in the way you treat the people you lead, and apologize?

Questions of the Habits

- *Solitude*—Are you ready to be with Me alone on a regular basis to keep things straight between us?
- *Prayer*—How can your prayer life be different so we can communicate on a regular basis?
- *Bible study*—Are you actively seeking My guidance through spending time in My Holy Word?
- *Experiencing God's unconditional love*—Do you sense God's unconditional love for you today?
- *Supportive relationships*—Do you have a small group of like-minded friends with whom you can be open and vulnerable?

Tool #2—Emergency Numbers for the Soul

Primary Use

To be an effective antidote to fear and pride in times of trial and temptation

Warning

For these antidotes to be effective, they need to be memorized in order to be available when needed. Saying them in an audible voice increases their effectiveness.

In Case of Fear

- "Be anxious for nothing, but in everything by prayer and supplication, with thanksgiving, let your requests be made known to God; and the peace of God, which surpasses all understanding, will guard your hearts and minds through Christ Jesus" (Philippians 4:6–7 NKJV).

- "The LORD is my shepherd; I shall not want. He makes me to lie down in green pastures; He leads me beside the still waters. He restores my soul; He leads me in the paths of righteousness for His name's sake. Yea, though I walk through the valley of the shadow of death, I will fear no evil; for You are with me; Your rod and Your staff, they comfort me. You prepare a table before me in the presence of my enemies. You anoint my head with oil; my cup runs over. Surely goodness and mercy will follow me all the days of my life, and I will dwell in the house of the LORD forever" (Psalm 23 NKJV).

In Case of Temptation

- "No temptation has overtaken you except such as is common to man; but God is faithful, who will not allow you to be tempted beyond what you are able, but with the temptation will also make the way of escape, that you may be able to bear it" (1 Corinthians 10:13 NKJV).

In Case of an Attack of Pride

- "For I say, through the grace given to me, to everyone who is among you, not to think of himself more highly than he ought to think, but to think soberly, as God has dealt to each one a measure of faith" (Romans 12:3 NKJV).

- "By pride comes nothing but strife, but with the well-advised is wisdom" (Proverbs 13:10 NKJV).

When You Need to Check Your Values

- "Thus says the LORD: 'Let not the wise man glory in his wisdom, let not the mighty man glory in his might, nor let the rich man glory in his riches; but let him who glories glory in this, that he understands and knows Me, that I am the LORD, exercising lovingkindness, judgment, and righteousness in the earth. For in these I delight,' says the LORD" (Jeremiah 9:23–24 NKJV).

When You Need to Take Accountability for a Mistake and Repent

- "If we confess our sins, He is faithful and just to forgive us our sins and to cleanse us from all unrighteousness" (1 John 1:9 NKJV).

When You Need Guidance

- "Trust in the LORD with all your heart, and lean not on your own understanding; in all your ways acknowledge Him, and He will direct your paths" (Proverbs 3:5–6 NKJV).
- "Teach me to do Your will, for You are my God; Your Spirit is good. Lead me in the land of uprightness" (Psalm 143:10 NKJV).

Tool #3—Power Drill for Uncovering Your True Leadership Motivation

Primary Use

To improve your awareness of what drives your willingness to serve as a leader by applying a measure of brutal honesty

Warning

What is uncovered through the use of this tool may not be pretty and may require extensive EGO realignment.

Instructions

One way to uncover the truth about your leadership motivations is to test your response to the question "Why do I lead?" by completing the sentence as many times in succession as you need to until you uncover the root cause of why you lead.

Example:

I coach Little League so that ____________________________

So that____________________________________

So that____________________________________

I serve as an elder in my church so that ____________________

So that____________________________________

So that ____________________________________

Jesus was absolutely transparent and always in touch with the root cause of all He did. "For I have come down from heaven not to do my will, but to do the will of him who sent me. And this is the will of him who sent me, that I shall lose none of all that he has given me, but raise them up at the last day" (John 6:38–39).

If your final response to the "So that . . ." question brings you to a point where your true motives for leading reflect a servant heart, then a productive next step would be to consider how to combat those temptations that can pull you away from following through on your good intentions. The answers will come from looking at the health of your habits in staying close to the transforming power of your relationship with the Father, the Son, and the Holy Spirit through the disciplines of solitude, prayer, study and application of Scripture, and having truth-tellers in your life.

Tool #4—Lead Like Jesus Personal Assessment and Action-Planning Guide

Directions

Step 1: Rate your consistency in applying the principles of *Lead Like Jesus* to your daily decisions and activities during the past week.

Step 2: From the four domains of leadership—*heart* (motivation), *head* (point of view), *hands* (behavior), and *habits* (spiritual renewal activities)—select one action area you want to focus on during the next two weeks.

Step 3: Share your action plans with at least one other person who is willing to act as your accountability and prayer partner.

Step 4: Write down your Lead Like Jesus goals on an index card so you can review your intentions throughout the week and as a reminder for specific prayer.

The Heart of the Servant Leader—Motivation

- I depended on the work of the Holy Spirit in my life and relationships.

  Rarely____Once in a while____Frequently____Consistently____

- I actively sought and encouraged feedback on my leadership.
  Rarely____Once in a while____Frequently____Consistently____

- I took personal risk to support and protect others.
  Rarely____Once in a while____Frequently____Consistently____

- I shared credit for the results of my group's efforts.
  Rarely____Once in a while____Frequently____Consistently____

- I avoided letting my EGO negatively impact my leadership this week.
  Rarely____Once in a while____Frequently____Consistently____

- The leadership motivation–related action I want to focus on for improvement during the next two weeks is ______________________
  ____

- I will accomplish the following specific action goal related to my leadership motivation during the next two weeks: ______________
  ____

The Head *of the Servant Leader—Leadership Point of View*

- I aligned my leadership point of view to that which I found in the Scriptures.
  Rarely____Once in a while____Frequently____Consistently____

- I treated growth and development of people as being equally important as producing results.
  Rarely____Once in a while____Frequently____Consistently____

- I developed, communicated, and reinforced a clear vision and set of rank-ordered operating values for my group.
  Rarely____Once in a while____Frequently____Consistently____

- I communicated my leadership point of view to members of my organization.
  Rarely____Once in a while____Frequently____Consistently____

- The leadership point of view–related action I want to focus on for improvement during the next two weeks is____________________
  ____

- I will accomplish the following specific action goal related to my leadership point of view during the next two weeks:
  ____
  ____

The Hands *of the Servant Leader—Leadership Behavior*

- I practiced the "not so with you" mandate of Jesus.
  Rarely____Once in a while____Frequently____Consistently____

- I tested for understanding and established clear performance goals when assigning tasks within my group.
  Rarely____Once in a while____Frequently____Consistently____

- I applied different leadership styles depending on the development level of the individuals assigned to perform specific tasks.
  Rarely____Once in a while____Frequently____Consistently____

- I praised progress and was actively engaged in day-to-day coaching.
  Rarely____Once in a while____Frequently____Consistently____

- I took positive action to resist the temptations to manipulate the fears and pride of others to get things done.
  Rarely____Once in a while____Frequently____Consistently____

- The leadership behavior–related action I want to focus on for improvement during the next two weeks is ____________________
  ____

- I will accomplish the following specific action goal related to my leadership behavior during the next two weeks:
  ____
  ____

The Habits *of the Servant Leader—Daily Recalibration*

- I called upon the Holy Spirit to guide my words, thoughts, actions, and behaviors.
  Rarely____Once in a while____Frequently____Consistently____

- I practiced the discipline of solitude.
  Rarely____Once in a while____Frequently____Consistently____

- I employed prayer as my first response instead of my last resort in meeting the challenges, temptations, and opportunities of the week.
  Rarely____Once in a while____Frequently____Consistently____

- I sought God's wisdom in the study and memorization of Scripture to stay focused on being a servant leader.
  Rarely____Once in a while____Frequently____Consistently____

- I maintained active accountability relationships to keep making progress on my good intentions as a servant leader.
  Rarely____Once in a while____Frequently____Consistently____

- The leadership habit I want to focus on for improvement during the next two weeks is ________________________________
  ____

- I will accomplish the following specific action goal related to my leadership habits during the next two weeks: ________________
  ____

A Prayer and Action Plan for the Upcoming Week

Heavenly Father, in full surrender to Your will and care, I pray, in the name of Jesus, for the power and the guidance of Your Holy Spirit to help me make these changes in my stewardship of influence opportunities that are placed in my path during the coming week. In the strong name of Jesus, amen!

Tool #5—Prayers for the Journey from Call to Commission

The Prayer of a Novice

Father, thank You for this chance to learn something new! As I seek to honor You by submitting to the instructions of my teacher, help me to approach the learning process with a teachable spirit. Help me to be patient with myself and with my teacher. Give me the courage to be willing to ask questions when things are not clear and not to be afraid to look a little foolish when trying things for the first time. Lord Jesus, help me to keep my pride in what I already know in check so I can learn what I don't know. As You were obedient when under instruction, help me to be obedient so that I may grow in wisdom and in my ability to serve You by serving others. In Jesus' name, amen!

Second Novice Prayer

Father, You know that this opportunity is something I am not looking forward to or excited about, yet here it is. Lord, help me see it as an opportunity to grow in endurance and grace and to be a witness of the strength that comes from You.

Lord Jesus, help me find new meaning in what I am assigned to do. Just as You learned and labored in this world at a common trade, help me remember to do all things for the glory of God. Speak to my heart, plant a new song in my mouth, but most of all, Father, teach me to trust You in the midst of this raging storm. I know that You will go before me, and in the dark night You will carry me. In You I put my trust. In Jesus' strong name, amen!

The Prayer of an Apprentice

Lord, I am learning a new task, and it's turning out to be harder than I thought! By now, I expected to know more about it than I do and be able to perform more on my own than I can. Lord, I don't want to fail, and I don't want to seem stupid or silly for asking questions for which I ought to know the answers. Help me accept the fact that everything may not come easily and that I have to be accountable for having a teachable attitude even when the going gets rough. Help me focus my thoughts, and take my anxiety from me. Teach me how to do this task in the right way with a patient and forgiving heart and to quickly apply the new learning so that I don't forget. In Jesus' name, amen!

Second Apprentice Prayer

Lord, this task seems harder than I thought it was. Maybe I'm not cut out to do it, but I know that You have faithfully brought me to this place and that You believe in me. Help me to believe in myself too! I want to do this assignment with the right heart and mind and to learn as much as I can, so remove my fears and false pride so that while learning, I can serve as well. I want to demonstrate You to those around me, so calm my mind and help me do this well. In Jesus' name, amen!

The Prayer of a Journeyman

Father, thank you for putting the teachers and experiences in my path that have brought me to this season of skill and experience where I am able to produce high-quality results from my personal efforts. Lord, thank you for allowing me to be excited about where my work fits in and that it has meaning. Because I have been at it a while, sometimes my enthusiasm and excitement about the work I do declines, and I get down on myself and others. Lord, help renew a right spirit in me. Help me regain a sense of purpose and stewardship of the gifts, talent, and opportunities You gave me. Help me be an encouragement to those who are in the learning process and to be a good model and witness for you. In Jesus' name, amen.

Second Journeyman Prayer

Lord, I don't know where to go from here. Because of some setbacks and mistakes I take responsibility for, I have lost some of my self-confidence and inspiration. I feel reluctant to step out of my comfort zone to teach others what I know or to act in a leadership position.

Lord, I know You have placed me here to be a light on a hill. Help me listen to wise counsel, be totally honest about my current situation, and be open to taking a positive step back to the level of service and commitment I once enjoyed under Your wings of mercy and grace. In Jesus' name, amen.

The Prayer of Master/Teacher

Lord, You have blessed me with the ability and opportunity to develop into a master of this role or task You put before me. You have walked with me through the growing process and have allowed me to remain humble enough and teachable enough to become an expert at this task. Help me now, Lord, to take what I have been given and use it to serve others by example and by sharing my knowledge with others. Lord, keep me ever mindful of the debt I owe to You and to those who taught me so well. Give me patience to faithfully and carefully teach those I serve and to avoid the temptation to become arrogant or complacent in my expertise. In Jesus' name, amen.

Second Master/Teacher Prayer

Lord, You know that I get tired and weary of teaching, leading, and serving those new to these tasks. I need Your strength, character, and perseverance to do this again. Help me see the reward in doing this because it is You that I serve. Let me nurture the enthusiasm of the novices and calm the fear of the apprentices. Give me patience to respond with excitement to their questions and concerns. Help me to not reflect an unhappy heart but a heart that is full of love and compassion for each one of them and their situation. Let the title of "master/teacher" remind me of my own Master and Teacher—the Lord Jesus! In His name, amen.

The Prayer of an Instructor of Novices

Father, today I greet a group of novices. For the most part, they are excited about their new assignment and eager to learn. Some already know something about their tasks, some know nothing, and some think they know things but they are the wrong things. As I face them, Father, give me the grace to love each one as You would.

Help me remember what it was like for me when I was just starting out and be sensitive to both their fears and lack of understanding of what is involved in learning this new task or role. Give me the wisdom to know what they need to know and clear thoughts as I consider each task to be taught. Help my presentation to be meaningful to each one so that learning will take place. Allow my face to reflect You rather than what I may feel about each question that is asked. Most of all, may they see in me a reflection of You. In Jesus' name, amen.

The Prayer of a Mentor of Apprentices

Father, today I will continue to guide the learning path of those I have committed to train in a set of specific skills. So far, they have progressed from unskilled novices to partially trained apprentices. Most of them have found the new work more difficult than anticipated. Some have voiced frustration and discouragement with themselves, with me, and with the whole learning process. Some, on the other hand, are overconfident and impatient to move on before they are really well prepared.

Lord, I will need patience and wisdom as I greet them today. Help me to remain sensitive to their individual needs. Some will need encouragement. Help me to see and praise their progress. Some will need to have their inflated pride in their initial accomplishments tempered with a sense of what they still need to learn. Help me to be patient but firm. May I faithfully teach the new tasks with skill, integrity, and wisdom and avoid delegating work prematurely.

Thanks, Father, for this opportunity to grow and develop in my own experiences as well as to teach others. I know that in this I am following the way of Jesus. In His name, amen.

The Prayer of an Inspirer of Journeymen

Father, today I am called to serve the needs of journeymen. These people know how to do a good job and have proven to be reliable individual performers. What I may be called on to provide is to help them reconnect with greater meaning and purpose or encourage them to perform it in a new environment. Maybe it will be to provide reassurance to someone who has suffered a setback that has made him question his own abilities.

Father, help me to be slow to speak, slow to offer advice or prescribe ready-made solutions. Help me to be patient and understanding. Guide my thoughts and actions in a way that the people I am seeking to help will be encouraged to draw on what they know and have experienced so they can make positive choices for their future. In Jesus' name, amen.

The Prayer of a Commissioner of Master/Teachers

Lord, what an awesome time! The people I have guided through the learning process have arrived at the point of being fully inspired and equipped not only to do the work on their own but also to serve and teach others. They have been entrusted to me for a little while, and I have faithfully imparted my knowledge to them and in that we both have grown. I have learned as much from them as they have learned from me. Father, help me send them from this learning experience with a sense of my confidence in them and appreciation for their teachable spirits. As You sent out Your apostles to spread the good news and assured them of Your constant availability, help me send my students with the same assurances. Lord, part of me doesn't want to let them go. I know some will experience difficulties, and some will reap rewards. Some will have to work harder than others, while some will have an easy time. Each is a unique individual created in Your image. Bless each one. In Jesus' name, amen.

In Conclusion

The world desperately needs new leadership role models, and Jesus has shown us the way to lead. Now that you have the tools to lead like Jesus, put them into practice. We wish you peace and joy on your journey. Remember, God is with you every step of the way.

Notes

Preface: *The Lead Like Jesus Journey*

1. Ken Blanchard and Norman Vincent Peale, *The Power of Ethical Management* (New York: William Morrow, 1988).

Chapter 1: Who Will You Follow? How Will You Lead?

1. William Barclay, *Barclay's Daily Study Bible* (NT) (Louisville, KY: John Knox Press, 1979).

Chapter 2: The *Heart* of a Servant Leader

1. Gordon MacDonald, *Ordering Your Private World* (Wheaton: Tyndale, 2003).
2. Leighton Ford, *Transforming Leadership: Jesus' Way of Creating Vision, Shaping Values and Empowering Change* (Downers Grove, Ill.: InterVarsity, 1991).
3. W. E. Vine, ed., *An Expository Dictionary of Biblical Words* (Nashville: Thomas Nelson, 1985), s.v. "Fear."
4. Robert S. McGee, *The Search for Significance: Seeing Your True Worth Through God's Eyes* (Nashville: W Publishing Group, 2003).
5. Jim Collins, *Good to Great: Why Some Companies Make the Leap . . . and Others Don't* (New York: HarperCollins, 2001).
6. Fred Smith, *You and Your Network* (Mechanicsburg, Penn.: Executive Books, 1998).
7. Alcoholics Anonymous, *The Big Book of Alcoholics Anonymous* (New York: Works Publishing, 1939).

Chapter 3—The *Head* of a Servant Leader

1. Noel Tichy with Eli Cohen, *The Leadership Engine* (New York: Harper Collins, 2002).
2. Ken Blanchard and Jesse Stoner, *Full Steam Ahead: The Power of Vision* (San Francisco: Berrett-Kohler, 2003).

Chapter 4—The *Hands* of a Servant Leader

1. Some translations render Mark 17:21 as "But this kind does not go out except by prayer and fasting."
2. Ken Blanchard first developed Situational Leadership® with Paul Hersey in the late 1960s. It was in the early 1980s that Blanchard and the Founding Associates of The Ken Blanchard Companies—Margie Blanchard, Don

Carew and Eunice Parisi-Carew, Fred Finch, Calla Crafts, Laurie Hawkins, and Pat and Drea Zigarmi—created a new generation of the theory called Situational Leadership® II. The best description of this thinking can be found in Kenneth Blanchard, Patricia Zigarmi, and Drea Zigarmi's *Leadership and the One Minute Manager* (New York: William Morrow, 1985.)

Chapter 5: The *Habits* of a Servant Leader

1. Rick Warren, *The Purpose Driven Life: What on Earth Am I Here For?* (Grand Rapids: Zondervan, 2002), 175.
2. *NIV Audio Bible* (Grand Rapids: Zondervan, 2002).
3. *The Visual Bible*, produced by GNN International Corp. and Visual Bible, LLC (2004), available for the books of Matthew and Acts.
4. From the *Following Jesus Project* (Richmond, Va.: International Mission Board, 2005). For more information, contact info@fjseries.org or go to http://FJseries.org.
5. Adapted from *The Disciple's Cross: MasterLife Discipleship Training for Leaders* (Nashville: LifeWay, 1996), 110–13.
6. Ken Blanchard, Bill Hybels, and Phil Hodges, *Leadership by the Book: Tools to Transform Your Workplace* (New York: William Morrow, 1999), 110.

Chapter 6—Why Should You Lead Like Jesus?

1. Adapted from Gene Hall and his colleagues at the University of Texas at Austin. See G. Hall and S. Hord, *Taking Charge of Change* (Austin, Tex.: Association for Curriculum Development, 1987); S. Loucks-Horsely and S. Steigelbauer, "Using Knowledge of Change to Guide Staff Development," *Staff Development for Education in the '90s: New Demands, New Realities, New Perspectives* (New York: Teachers College Press, 1991).
2. Jim Collins, *From Good to Great: Why Some Companies Make the Leap and Others Don't* (New York: HarperCollins, 2001).
3. Barbara Gellerman, "How Bad Leadership Happens," *Leader to Leader* no. 35 (Winter 2005): 41–46.
4. Drea Zigarmi, Ken Blanchard, et al, *The Leader Within* (Upper Saddle River, N.J.: Pearson Education, 2005).
5. Bob Buford and Terry Whalin, *Halftime: Changing Your Game Plan from Success to Significance* (Grand Rapids: Zondervan, 1994).
6. Lloyd John Ogilve, *The Bush is Still Burning* (Dallas: Word, 1980).
7. Henry and Richard Blackaby, *Spiritual Leadership* (Nashville: Broadman and Holman, 2001).

Discussion Guide

Welcome to the *Lead Like Jesus* discussion guide!

To help enrich your understanding and application of the wonderful leadership principles that are part of your inheritance as a follower of Jesus, we have prepared a summary of key concepts contained in each of the six chapters of *Lead Like Jesus.* The key concepts are followed by a series of discussion questions to stimulate your thinking and conversation about how to bring leading like Jesus into all of your important relationships.

We want to encourage you to proceed through this discussion guide at your own pace. Don't make it into something to check off on another "been there, done that" to-do list.

This interactive discussion guide is designed primarily for use in a group setting, which we highly recommend, but is also useful for individual study. We hope that by reading *Lead Like Jesus* and sharing the learning experience with others you will not only acquire a deeper understanding of what leading like Jesus is all about but will be inspired to apply the principles in your daily leadership opportunities.

Picture yourself and those you are sharing this experience with as going on a relaxing walk, with Jesus stopping along the way to ask and answer questions in a completely loving and secure environment.

Listen to Him as He calls your name and says to you once more, "Come to me, all you who are weary and burdened, and I will give you rest. Take my yoke upon you and learn from Me, for I am gentle and humble in heart, and you will find rest for your souls. For My yoke is easy and My burden is light" (Matthew 11:28–30).

Blessings to you as you Lead like Jesus,
Ken Blanchard and Phil Hodges

Chapter 1
Who Will You Follow? How Will You Lead?

Key Concept: (Pages 3–11)

Leadership is a **process of influence**. Anytime you seek to influence the thinking, behavior, or development of people in their personal or professional lives, you are taking on the role of a leader.

Discussion Questions:

1. Think of two situations in which you currently act in a leadership role: one as an organizational leader and one in a life role leadership situation. How are these leadership roles different and how are they alike?
2. What basic question do you have to answer if you are going to seek to lead like Jesus in both of these situations?
3. What is it about each of these leadership roles that makes it difficult to follow through on seeking to serve rather than to be served?

Key Concept: (Pages 12–19)

Jesus called them together and said, "You know the rulers of the Gentiles lord it over them, and their high officials exercise authority over them. **Not so with you.** Instead, whoever wants to be great among you must be your servant, and whoever wants to be first must be your slave—just as the Son of Man did not come to be served, but to serve, and to give his life as a ransom for many."
—Matthew 20:25–28, emphasis added

Discussion Questions:

1. Jesus called his followers to exhibit a radically different approach to leadership than was being exhibited in the world around them. As a modern-day follower of Jesus, how would you describe the general pattern of leadership you have observed and experienced in today's society?

2. Is the servant leadership that Jesus expected from his followers any more or less radical today than it was in the first century? Why?

3. How do you think Jesus would modify his instructions to modern leaders, given the complexity and potential impact of their leadership decisions on a global economy?

4. Given his mandate to serve rather than be served and his practical experience in the day-to-day issues of leadership, name three ways Jesus would approach your leadership responsibilities differently than you do.

Key Concept: (Pages 19–30)

Learning to lead like Jesus is more than to an announcement; it is a commitment to lead in a different way. It is a **transformational cycle** that begins with personal leadership, moves to leading others in one-on-one relationships, then to leading a team or group, and finally, to leading an organization or community.

Discussion Questions:

1. Leadership isn't something that you do to people. It is something that you do with people that answers the questions "Whose are you?" and "Who are you?" How will knowing the answer to those questions impact the nature of your leadership of others?

2. What portions of the Transformed Personal Lead Like Jesus Perspective (pp. 23–24) most closely reflects your own perspective, and what portions seem the most distant to you at this moment?

3. Name three ways you nurture trust in one-on-one relationships at work and at home.

4. Discuss a time when you lost trust in a leader and how it impacted your relationship.

5. How do you think people in your family would describe your leadership in the following situations?

A time of crisis
A time of failure
A time of victory
A time of plenty
A time of want

6. What is most likely to occur when leaders try to drive change at the organizational level without first addressing the issue of their own credibility at the personal, one-on-one, and team leadership levels?

Key Concept: (Pages 31–35)

Leading like Jesus involves the alignment of **four leadership domains**: *heart*, *head*, *hands*, and *habits*. The internal domains—the motivations of your *heart* and the leadership perspectives of your *head*—are things you can keep inside or even disguise if it suits your purpose. The external domains—your public leadership behavior, or *hands*, and your *habits* as experienced by others—will determine whether people will follow you.

1. Briefly describe in your own words what is meant by the terms *heart*, *head*, *hands*, and *habits* of leadership.

2. What was your biggest "Aha!" in reading Chapter One, and how do you plan to use your insight in seeking to lead like Jesus?

3. What will be your first step toward putting this "Aha!" into action? Your second step? Your third?

4. What will keep you from moving forward? How can you remove this barrier?

Chapter 2
The Heart of the Servant Leader

Key Concept: (Pages 39–45)
The most persistent barrier to leading like Jesus is a heart motivated by **self-interest**.

Discussion Questions:

1. In which of the following situations are you most prone to put your own agenda ahead of those you lead?

____ At work
____ At home
____ In your marriage or friendships
____ In your volunteer activities

2. Why do you think this happens?

3. Which of the following words best describes your usual reaction to feedback on your performance?

Fear __	Anger__	Denial__	Sadness___
Curiosity___	Gratitude___	Humility__	Pride___

4. What would your daily, weekly, quarterly, or yearly calendar reveal regarding how you view the importance of preparing others to take your place when the time comes?

Key Concept: (Pages 48–63)

If, as a leader, you want to follow the mandate Jesus gave us—to serve rather than be served—you have to realize that every day you will face all kinds of challenges to your good intentions. Our adversary consistently tries to get us to be self-serving. To resist the temptation to be drawn off course, we must understand the dynamics of a self-serving **EGO** that **Edges God Out**.

Discussion Questions:

1. List three things that people worship in our modern society and look toward to provide them with security and a sense of identity other than God. How stable and trustworthy are each of the things you listed as a permanent source of security and self-worth in a changing world?

2. If your sense of self-worth is tied to how well you perform and the opinion of other people, how are you likely to react when your performance isn't good enough or if people don't agree or approve of your actions?

3. Think of a time when your pride may have prevented you from admitting to a mistake or apologizing to someone you had treated badly. How did it make you feel? What did it do to your relationship?

4. Which of the following fears are most likely to prevent you from following through on your good intentions or create a tendency toward a fight-or-flight mentality when confronted with an uncomfortable decision?

Fear of rejection____	Fear of failure___
Fear of inadequacy___	Fear of intimacy___
Fear of death___	Fear of the future___
Fear of success___	Fear of want___
Fear of loneliness___	Fear of pain___
Fear of loss of control___	Fear of ridicule___
Fear of losing___	Fear of conflict___
Fear of humiliation___	Fear of tests___
Fear of public speaking___	

5. Describe a situation in which your fears overtook your good intentions and the result.

Key Concept: (Pages 63–75)

The mirror image of Edging God Out is **Exalting God Only**. The key to this transformation is altaring your leadership EGO. *Altaring* is not misspelled. That's exactly what you have to do—put your EGO on the altar and exalt God only.

Discussion Questions:

1. What do you think the impact of your leadership and relationships would be if your pride and fears were replaced with humility and God-grounded confidence?

2. What is it about your current concept of and relationship with God that might be blocking you from accepting His unconditional love and promises as the source of your security and self-worth?

3. The hardest step to recovery is the first one of admitting that you have a problem you can't fix on your own and asking for help.

Have you taken that first step regarding your leadership EGO, and if not, why?

Key Concept: (Pages 76–79)

What does seeking first the kingdom of God mean in terms of our leadership decisions? It means bringing an **eternal perspective** into the realm of practical, day-to-day leadership decisions that effects better results and relationships. It means revising the way we see people, situations, and priorities to the way God sees them, and inviting the Holy Spirit into our relationships to infuse into our thoughts and actions two key elements of leading like Jesus—forgiveness and grace.

Discussion Questions:

1. Why is forgiveness an important aspect of leadership?
2. What is the price that must be paid if true forgiveness is to have an impact on the future of a relationship?
3. Whom do you need to forgive in order to restore a relationship with someone who let you down?
4. Describe in your own words what it means, as a leader, to extend grace to someone under your influence.
5. What was your biggest "Aha!" in reading Chapter Two, and how do you plan to use your insight in seeking to lead like Jesus?
6. What will be your first step toward putting this "Aha!" into action? Your second step? Your third?
7. What will keep you from moving forward? How can you remove this barrier?

Chapter 3
The Head of a Servant Leader

Key Concept: (Pages 83–98)

Leadership is about going somewhere. Effective leadership begins with a **clear vision**, whether for your personal life, your family, or an organization. If your followers don't know where you are going and where you are trying to take them, they will have a hard time getting excited about the journey.

Discussion Questions:

1. Describe what "business you are in" as a person, as an organizational leader, as a life role leader, and as follower of Jesus. Is it the same "business" or does it differ from one situation to another, and if so, why?
2. Describe what your preferred view of the future will look like if you are successful in your life purpose and relationships?
3. Imagine you are being interviewed by your ten-year-old daughter and she asks you, "What are the four most important rules in our family?" What would your answer be?

Key Concept: (Pages 99–106)

Once people have a picture of where you want to take them and why, the leadership emphasis switches to the second role of leadership—**implementation**. The leader now becomes, in a sense, a servant of the vision, by serving the people who are being asked to act according to the vision and accomplish the goals.

Discussion Questions:

1. Imagine what the disciples experienced as their Lord and Teacher humbled Himself and performed such a personal and intimate service as washing their feet. What images come to mind from your own life of someone you know performing an act of humble service leadership? For example, think of a mother with a newborn child.

2. Describe a situation when the response you received for service resembled the quacking of ducks in a duck pond. "It's our policy." (*Quack, Quack*). "Don't blame me; I just work here." (*Quack, Quack*). "Would you like to speak to my supervisor?" (*Quack, Quack.*) Who bears the responsibility for creating "duck ponds"?

3. What steps could you take to change a situation from quacking like ducks to soaring like eagles?

Key Concept: (Pages 108–115)

One of the greatest services a leader can provide to his or her followers is **constancy of purpose**. When the going gets rough or temptations and distractions come with short-term success or setbacks, people will look to their leaders to see how they will respond. Will they stay on course and remain true to their mission and values, or will they give up and give in to the pressures of the moment?

Discussion Questions:

1. Think of a time in your life when a leader you were following stayed strong and on purpose even in the face of tremendous pressure to give up and give in. What was the long-range impact on your desire to follow and trust that leader?

2. Describe some of the internal and external pressures that Jesus withstood in completing the ultimate service on our behalf.

3. As a leader, list three things that are most likely to pull you off course. What impact does changing course or direction have on the morale of the people you lead?

4. Describe in your own words the two parts of leadership—vision and implementation—and the role of the leader in creating an environment where people get excited about where they are headed and how they are going to get there.

5. What was your biggest "Aha!" in reading Chapter Three, and how do you plan to use your insight in seeking to lead like Jesus?

6. What will be your first step toward putting this "Aha!" into action? Your second step? Your third?

7. What will keep you from moving forward? How can you remove this barrier?

Chapter 4
The Hands of the Servant Leader

Key Concept: (Pages 119–126)

A key activity of an effective servant leader is to act as a **performance coach**. When Jesus called His disciples to follow Him, He pledged them His full support and guidance as they developed into "fishers of men." This is the duty of a servant leader—the ongoing investment of the leader's life into the lives of those who follow. There are three parts to becoming a performance coach: performance planning, day-to-day coaching, and performance evaluation. When any one of the three elements is missing, everyone suffers the consequences.

Discussion Questions:

1. If there is not clear communication of what a good job will look like when it is accomplished, somebody will end up frustrated—either the leader or the follower or both. Describe a time when you were on either side of a failure in communication on what was expected and what was delivered. Recall the frustration and wasted energy that could have been avoided by testing for understanding.

2. It is only through day-to-day coaching that a leader ensures that the dual goals of positive results and relationships are accomplished. Jesus spent the majority of His season of earthly leadership teaching, modeling, and redirecting His disciples until they were equipped to carry on without His physical presence. Only then did He send them out. List three things that happen when a leader delegates responsibility and fails to provide help and guidance along the way.

Key Concept: (Pages 127–139)

To progress from being a novice to becoming a master in any role or skill, learners need **someone to guide them** along the way and to give them what they need to advance through the learning process.

Discussion Questions:

1. Describe a time when you were an untrained novice just starting to learn a new task or role. What did you need most from someone else to help you get started? Did you get it? If not, what was the result?

2. Describe an apprentice time when you were in the process of learning something new and needed someone to push you beyond a

failure or an easy success to get to a higher level of understanding and performance. Think of a time when you quit because nobody was there to take you to the next level.

3. Can you remember a time when you felt underappreciated for a job well done because all the attention was being given to the "problem children"? What would have been the effect of a leader reinforcing you with some small heartfelt sign of appreciation?

4. Sending someone out to act on your behalf is the highest form of validation of your trust in that person's competence and commitment. Describe a time when you were given the opportunity to teach and guide others in what you had been taught. How did the way you were prepared as a follower impact how you lead others?

Key Concept: (Pages 140–150)

The true test of servant leadership begins when the EGO of the leader and the EGO of the follower **engage** one another. How well they recognize and overcome the pride and fears in their relationship determines whether they move toward mutual satisfactions of commonly held goals or share in frustrations of their own making.

Discussion Questions:

1. The ideal, most productive relationship between a leader and a follower occurs when a servant-hearted leader and a servant-hearted follower engage one another in an atmosphere of mutual service and trust. Can you remember a situation when, as a leader or a follower, you felt this type of relationship occur between you and another person? What were the behaviors that helped produce a positive result and relationship?

2. When a leader and a follower are fearful of one another, what is most likely to happen? Give an example that you have observed or experienced.

3. What steps can you take to remove fear from a situation as a follower? As a leader?

4. When a leader and a follower are both caught up in their own pride and self importance, what is the impact on their productivity in producing results?

5. When prideful leaders exploit the fears of their followers to produce short-term results, what is likely to be the long-term impact on the level of commitment and enthusiasm for the task? Explain.

6. What was your biggest "Aha!" in reading Chapter Four, and how do you plan to use your insight in seeking to lead like Jesus?

7. What will be your first step toward putting this "Aha!" into action? Your second step? Your third?

8. What will keep you from moving forward? How can you remove this barrier?

Chapter 5
The Habits of a Servant Leader

Key Concept: (Pages 153–159)

As Jesus moved through His season of earthly leadership, He was under constant pressure and temptation to get off course or respond to the failings of both His friends and His enemies. Jesus stayed on track with His mission by applying five key habits that countered the negative forces in His life. Of the five habits we will discuss,

solitude is by far the most elusive in our modern world of busyness and 24-7 communication.

Discussion Questions:

1. When was the last time you spent a significant amount of time in solitude on purpose without a to-do, think, or pray list and sat quietly in God's presence listening to His "still small voice"? Describe your experience and what was going on before and after you took time out from doing things for God to just be with God.
2. What are the biggest barriers to your times of solitude, and what has worked for you in overcoming them?

Key Concept: (Pages 159–165)

If solitude is the most elusive of the habits for us to develop, **prayer** is the one that requires the most unlearning and revision of old habits and patterns. One of the most revealing questions you could ask a leadership candidate is "How is your prayer life?" The answer will speak volumes about where and how the leader might lead.

Discussion Questions:

1. How would you describe your prayer life in terms of when, what, where, how, and why? What are the best parts and those that need improvement?
2. What do you think would be the impact on how you approached the people or circumstances involved, if the next time you faced an important challenge or temptation, you prayed for them, not about them, beforehand?
3. Take a moment and, using the ACTS model, focus on one thing you **A**dore about God; one thing you need to **C**onfess to God;

one thing for which you are Thankful to God; and one thing you want to request from God in Supplication. Repeat this process as often throughout the day as you need to—God never gets tired of the conversation.

Key Concept: (Pages 165–174)

It is well and good to know that the **Bible** is useful, reliable, and valuable. It is another thing to make it your own in a practical way. The Bible is a love letter written to you from your Father.

Discussion Questions:

1. Which of the following methods of becoming familiar with God's Word do you most often rely on? What are the advantages and disadvantages you have experienced in putting what you have learned into practice in a time of need?

Listening to the Word
Reading the Word
Studying the Word
Memorizing the Word
Meditating on the Word

2. Remember a time when you were faced with a decision and your knowledge of Scripture made a difference in what you chose to do? What was the result?

Key Concept: (Pages 175–179)

When you cast off your doubts and reservations about **God's love** and accept that you can't earn it, don't deserve it, and can't add to it or lose it, you can proceed in that reality to live and lead in confidence, humility, and true freedom.

Discussion Questions:

1. Think of a time when, beyond a shadow of a doubt, you experienced God's love for you personally, specifically, and in a way that only He and you knew its true significance in your life. How did you feel at the time? How do you feel at this moment? What do you need to say to God?

2. What do you think would be the first improvement in your leadership and relationships if you were able to cast off your fears and your pride and replace them with God-grounded confidence and humility?

Key Concept: (Pages 179–188)

Leadership can be a lonely business filled with great amounts of soul-draining human interaction but little soul-filling intimacy. Without some **safe-harbor relationships** where we can lay down all the armor and weapons we need to face the world and relax in confidence and unguarded communion, we become vulnerable to two debilitating frames of mind and spirit—the victim and the martyr.

Discussion Questions:

1. Who are the "truth tellers" in your life, the people who you depend on to love and accept you, warts and all, and to tell you what you need to know that you may not want to hear?

2. List three things that you do to make it easy for your truth tellers to help you and three things that you do that make it difficult for them to get through to you?

3. Who in your life are looking to you as their truth teller? How are you doing in watching their backs?

4. What was your biggest "Aha!" in reading Chapter Five, and how do you plan to use your insight in seeking to lead like Jesus?

5. What will be your first step toward putting this "Aha!" into action? Your second step? Your third?

6. What will keep you from moving forward? How can you remove this barrier?

Chapter 6
Why Lead Like Jesus?

Key Concept: (Pages 191–196)

As a philosophy of leadership, servant leadership may be considered one option among many others; but as a theology of leadership, it is a mandate for all who call Jesus Lord. Foundational to tapping into the essence of leading like Jesus is **embracing a life purpose** of loving God and loving and serving people.

Discussion Questions:

1. Soren Kirkegaard once noted, "If you don't seek first the kingdom of God, you will never seek it." How do you intend to take this caution seriously as you seek to lead like Jesus?

2. What three pieces of evidence would you rely on as proof of your commitment to lead like Jesus? Is it hard evidence found in action or merely circumstantial based on a nonspecific statement of future intent?

3. Think of a time when doing the loving thing instead of the popular thing, the easiest thing, or the safest thing would have restored or retained trust. Remember it for future reference.

Key Concept: (Pages 197–201)

From a practical point of view, servant leadership best serves the dual objectives of effective leadership—**results and relationships**.

Discussion Questions:

1. Which of the following effects of servant leadership most directly applies to the legacy you would like to leave behind when your season of influence is completed and why?

_____ Improved service to your customers

_____ Enhanced development of the talents and gifts of the people under your influence

_____ A more significant impact on the world around you

2. List two action steps you are willing to commit to take in the next thirty days to make this desired improvement a reality.

Key Concept: (Pages 202–214)

Leading like Jesus is not a course; it is a lifestyle. Making the development of people an equal partner with performance is a decision you make. It is following the example of Jesus as a servant leader and pouring your life into the lives of other people. It is about leaving a **leadership legacy of service**.

Discussion Questions:

1. If there were three words that survived fifty years from today to describe the legacy you left in the hearts and minds of those you served, what would you like them to be and why?

2. How would leading like Jesus improve the chances of securing a "Well done, good and faithful servant" at the end of your life's journey?

3. What was your biggest "Aha!" in reading Chapter Six, and how do you plan to use your insight in seeking to lead like Jesus?

4. What will be your first step toward putting this "Aha!" into action? Your second step? Your third?

5. What will keep you from moving forward? How can you remove this barrier?

Chapter 7
Next Steps to Lead like Jesus

Key Concept: (Pages 217–227)

Leading like Jesus is a daily journey and challenge rather than a final destination. It can be done only in and through the power of the Holy Spirit in your life and committed relationships, first with God and then with others. The journey of leading like Jesus will always be filled with failures, roughly right behaviors, and out-and-out victories. Staying the course means frequently checking where you are and where you are headed and making necessary **course corrections**.

Discussion Questions:

1. List one action item for each of the four leadership domains that you feel will be the hardest for you to improve consistently without the help of the Holy Spirit, and describe the nature of the obstacle you will face in trying.

Heart
Head
Hands
Habits

Key Concept: (Pages 228–234)

One unique resource at the disposal of the followers of Jesus is the **active participation of the Holy Spirit** as Counselor and Guide. Jesus promised in John 14:26, "The Counselor, the Holy Spirit, whom the Father will send in my name, will teach you all things and will remind you of everything I have said to you."

Discussion Question:

1. In your own words write a prayer to God and invite the Holy Spirit to take control of your *heart*, *head*, *hands*, and *habits* as you seek to gain victory over the barriers you mentioned above and to lead like Jesus. Repeat this process often and consistently. God Bless.